Policy Reform for
Sustainable Development in Africa

A Project of the

IISA Institut International des Sciences Administratives

IIAS International Institute of Administrative Sciences

Policy Reform for Sustainable Development in Africa

THE INSTITUTIONAL IMPERATIVE

edited by
Louis A. Picard
and Michele Garrity

Lynne Rienner Publishers ∎ Boulder & London

Published in the United States of America in 1994 by
Lynne Rienner Publishers, Inc.
1800 30th Street, Boulder, Colorado 80301

and in the United Kingdom by
Lynne Rienner Publishers, Inc.
3 Henrietta Street, Covent Garden, London WC2E 8LU

Library of Congress Cataloging-in-Publication Data
Policy reform for sustainable development in Africa : the
  institutional imperative / edited by Louis A. Picard and Michele
  Garrity.
      p.   cm.
  Includes bibliographical references and index.
  ISBN 1-55587-449-5 (alk. paper)
  1. Structural adjustment (Economic policy)—Africa—Case studies.
2. Sustainable development—Africa—Case studies.   3. Africa—
Politics and government—1960-   —Case studies.   I. Picard, Louis
A.   II. Garrity, Michele, 1951–
HC800.P634   1993
338.96—dc20   93–14601
                                                        CIP

British Cataloguing in Publication Data
A Cataloguing in Publication record for this book
is available from the British Library.

Printed and bound in the United States of America

The paper used in this publication meets the requirements
of the American National Standard for Permanence of
Paper for Printed Library Materials Z39.48–1984.

Contents

Foreword

Turkia Ould Daddah

Capacity building for policy change and sustainability is a subject now seriously confronting most Third World countries, as well as the organizations and agencies engaged in bilateral and multilateral development aid. This is one reason the International Institute of Administrative Sciences (IIAS) believed it would be worthwhile to bring together African academics and high-ranking civil servants to work, reflect, and exchange their views on this matter. Moreover, IIAS believes that the experience of these Africans in positions of responsibility and their knowledge of national realities enables them to provide information and ideas to political decisionmakers, senior managers, and international donors in the field of institutional development.

IIAS's main concern is to help improve the provision of government services, both nationally and internationally, by supporting a comparative study of administrative phenomena. The leadership of the institute believes that we are living in an era dominated by challenges of a global magnitude. Administrators cannot afford to ignore these challenges; rather, they must adapt to them by adjusting their structures and procedures.

The views of the African contributors expressed in this book as well as Louis A. Picard and Michele Garrity's analyses are not meant to be an exhaustive study of all facets of institutional capacity vis-à-vis change and support for public policies. However, the contributors unanimously recognize that the solutions and their implementation will not stem from reforms confined to their administrative and technical aspects, or by taking a solely economic and financial approach. We now know that the administrative and technical approach erred by advocating abstract standards of efficiency designed for economic, social, and cultural conditions that are not reflective of African countries. Structural adjustment programs, with their emphasis on the macro aspects of economic policy, have often ignored the administrative aspects of policy reform.

The readers may judge for themselves the results of this dialogue between academics and top-ranking African civil servants on an issue whose importance is widely recognized, and where the stakes concern every African state and the international community at large.

I extend warm thanks to Louis A. Picard, who put his knowledge and expertise at the disposal of IIAS for a working group oriented toward action. I also want to thank the African Association for Public Administration and Management (AAPAM) for agreeing to support and work with IIAS, thus allowing IIAS to benefit from their wide experience in Africa. Many thanks also to the Commonwealth Secretariat, which gave financial backing to this workshop intended to be an African contribution to the institutional development of the countries concerned.

Turkia Ould Daddah
Director General
International Institute of Administrative Sciences

Acknowledgments

The editors would like to express their appreciation for the support given to them in this project by Carlos Almada and Turkia Ould Daddah, former and current directors general of the International Institute of Administrative Sciences (IIAS), Brussels, Belgium. The workshop in Arusha, Tanzania, was cosponsored by the African Association for Public Administration and Management (AAPAM), then under the able directorship of Gelase Mutahaba, now of the Commonwealth Secretariat and the government of Tanzania.

Funding for this project came from the IIAS; the Commonwealth Secretariat; the European Centre for Development Policy Management (ECDPM); the AAPAM; the Graduate School of Public and International Affairs, the Office of Research, and the University Center for International Studies of the University of Pittsburgh; the American Consortium for International Public Administration; and the government of Tanzania. Our thanks to: Mohan Kaul, director of the Commonwealth Secretariat; Joan Corkery of the European Centre for Development Policy Management; Alfred Zuck, executive director of the National Association of Schools of Public Affairs and Administration and then president of IIAS; and Jeanne North, Office of Rural and Institutional Development, U.S. Agency for International Development (USAID). The Implementing Policy Change Project of USAID provided travel support for U.S. participants to the Arusha workshop.

The following individuals from the government of Tanzania assisted in the organization of the Arusha workshop: Ambassador Paul Rupia, secretary to the cabinet; Joseph A. Rugumyamheto, head of the secretariat; S. H. Kasori, A. H. Milanzi, Stephen

Mkokota, all of the President s Office; and Antipas Mwakila and Santiel S. Mbajo of the Regional Development Office in Arusha.

The following people attended the conference and/or assisted in the preparation of the proceedings: Vida Yeboah, Ministry of Education, Accra, Ghana; S. K. Wanjohi, National Management Policy Development Project, Nairobi, Kenya; M. N. Biam, Nigerian Military Government, Makurdi, Nigeria; Markka Kiviniemi, Finnish Technical Assistance Agency; Joan Corkery, European Centre for Development Policy Management, Maastricht, Netherlands; Colin Baker, University of Cardiff, UK; Bernard Mulokozi, chair, Civil Service Commission, Dar es Salaam, Tanzania; Joan Mbuya, government of Tanzania; Pat Isman, USAID; Ben Crosby, Management Systems International, Washington, D.C.; Eric Nelson, Development Alternatives, Washington, D.C.; Muhamed Aboud, auditor general, government of Tanzania, Dar es Salaam; Byarugaba E. Foster, Makerere University, Kampala, Uganda; and L. D. Mpande, Eastern and Southern Africa Management Institute, Arusha, Tanzania.

At IIAS, Brussels, we also wish to thank Catherine Bourtembourg, deputy director general, and Francisca Sabbe and Maximin Emagna, research assistants.

Our thanks also go to the following people, who helped in the preparation of this manuscript: Karen Jewell, Regan Petrie, Valarie Staats, Maureen Widsgowski, Joyce Valiquette, and Anita Tilford of the University of Pittsburgh, and Rosemarie Sigg and Linda Soisson, Johnstown, Pennsylvania.

Finally, the editors thank Lynne Rienner and her associates at Lynne Rienner Publishers for their support.

Louis A. Picard
Michele Garrity

Acronyms

AAPAM	African Association for Public Administration and Management
ACBI	Africa Capacity Building Initiative
AFRC	Armed Forces Revolution Council (Ghana)
AFRC	Armed Forces Ruling Council (Nigeria)
ASCON	Administrative Staff College of Nigeria
BDC	Botswana Development Corporation
BDP	Botswana Democratic Party
CCM	Chama Cha Mapinduzi (Tanzania)
CESAG	Centre Africain D'Etudes Supérieures en Gestion (Senegal)
CIPE	Center for International Private Enterprise
DDC	District Development Committee (Kenya)
DPMC	Development Program Management Center (U.S.)
EDI	Economic Development Institute (World Bank)
EEC	European Economic Community
ERP	Economic Recovery Program (Ghana)
ESAMI	Eastern and Southern African Management Institute
FEC	Federal Executive Council (Nigeria)
GDP	gross domestic product
GIMPA	Ghana Institute of Management and Public Administration
GOK	Government of Kenya
GTZ	German Technical Cooperation
IBRD	International Bank for Reconstruction and Development

IDM	Institute of Development Management
IIAS	International Institute of Administrative Sciences
ILO	International Labour Organisation
IMF	International Monetary Fund
IMTC	Inter-Ministerial Technical Committee (Tanzania)
INCAE	Central American Institute of Business
KANU	Kenya African National Union
LDCs	less developed countries
LGSM	Local Government Service Management (Botswana)
MADREC	Management Development Resource Center
MAN	Manufacturers' Association of Nigeria
MDPI	Management Development and Productivity Institute (Ghana)
MRU	Management Resource Unit
MSD	Mechanical Services Department (Zambia)
NAFTA	North American Free Trade Agreement
NASPAA	National Association of Schools of Public Affairs and Administration
NCDP	National Commission for Development Planning (Zambia)
NEC	National Executive Committee (Tanzania)
NEMIC	National Employment, Manpower and Incomes Advisory Board (Botswana)
NGOs	nongovernmental organizations
NICs	newly industrializing countries
NIPSS	National Institute for Policy and Strategic Studies (Nigeria)
NLC	National Liberation Council (Ghana)
NRC	National Redemption Council (Ghana)
OMS&T	Office of Management Services and Training (Nigeria)
PACC	Policy Analysis and Coordination Center (Ghana)
PARDIC	Public Administration Restructuring and Decentralisation Implementation Committee (Ghana)
PNDC	Provisional National Defence Council (Ghana)
PNP	People's National Party (Ghana)
PP	Progress Party (Ghana)
PVO	private voluntary organization
RFP	request for proposal
RTC	Regional Training Council
SADC	Southern African Development Council
SADCC	Southern African Development Coordination Conference

SAPAM	Special Action Programme in Administration and Management (UN)
SMC	Supreme Military Council (Ghana)
SOEs	state-owned enterprises
SRBC	SADCC Regional Business Council
UBLS	University of Botswana, Lesotho and Swaziland
UBS	University of Botswana and Swaziland
ULGS	Unified Local Government Service (Botswana)
UNDP	United Nations Development Programme
UNEDIL	UNDP/EDI/ILO project
UNESCO	United Nations Educational, Scientific, and Cultural Organisation
UNIP	United National Independence Party (Zambia)
USAID	United States Agency for International Development
ZIMCO	Zambia Industrial and Mining Corporation

1

The Challenge of
Structural Adjustment

Louis A. Picard

In the wake of the transformation of Eastern Europe and the former Soviet Union, many governments throughout the world are in various stages of economic and political transition.[1] For the less developed countries (LDCs), the hallmarks of this transition include a more prominent role for the market in economic development and a shift from highly centralized government to greater autonomy for intermediate and primary units of government. In Western Europe and North America, the transition is characterized by historical agreements to promote greater economic integration, such as the Maastricht Treaty and the North American Free Trade Agreement (NAFTA).

Although the economic dimensions of these efforts are fairly easy to discern—increased output, improved products and services, reduced trade barriers, competitive prices, higher and improved standards of living—the political dimensions of the transition are far from clear. Particularly in the less developed countries, the movement to privatize large sections of the economy and to decentralize government functions has produced lingering questions about the fundamental nature of the developmental state and the appropriate role for the state in a pluralistic, decentralized, market-oriented economy.[2] Mounting evidence from the Asian "tigers" and the newly industrializing countries (NICs) of Latin America strongly suggests that the state has played a more active role in the development process than was previously recognized.[3] This evidence has been further buttressed by recent case studies from the industrialized countries emphasizing the high-profile role of the state in the economic success of Japan and Germany.[4]

Clearly, "getting prices right" and the "free" and "unhindered" flow of goods and services within and between countries is proving to be more difficult than was once anticipated. As time and experiences accumulate, economic "miracles" are being increasingly understood in terms of an interwoven series of complex activities carried out by both the public sector and the private sector. Further, underlying these activities is a shared set of values, attitudes, and assumptions that reflect national character traits and beliefs, the political will to accomplish difficult objectives, a belief in the legitimacy of those charged with the nation's development, and, among the general public, a widespread trust in their chosen leadership.

Such intangibles imply there is much more to the development process than mere consideration of the best "mix" of trade- and investment-related policies, establishing the optimum exchange rate, and reducing debt-ratio levels. At issue are also questions of governance involving degrees of openness, levels of transparency, and accountability; a definition of roles for the public and private sectors in the decisionmaking process; and the appropriate legal and institutional framework for the planning, implementation, and monitoring of policy decisions.

Structural Adjustment Programs

In the years since 1979, the most common approach to assisting LDCs encountering serious macroeconomic problems has been the structural adjustment program, administered by the International Monetary Fund (IMF). As a response to a widespread excess of international indebtedness, the IMF often found itself in the position of having to institute quick and effective remedies to satisfy a country's creditors and to immediately stabilize the debtor country's economy. IMF activities of this nature quickly resulted in an off-the-shelf package of fiscal and monetary measures that were routinely implemented in one country after another with little regard for country-specific noneconomic conditions.[5] Two regions in particular were most heavily hit by excess debt problems: Africa—where countries are characterized by high levels of dependence on public funds from donor countries; and Latin America—where debt was largely accumulated through private financial markets.[6]

In Africa, governments have been operating under strict structural adjustment programs for almost ten years. Similar to the Latin American experience, these programs have consisted of two main components: stabilization policies and policy reform efforts. Stabilization efforts to reduce the current account balance and facilitate export trade necessitated bridging loans from the IMF to address the immediate domestic needs of debt management. Further stabilization requirements included reductions in domestic absorption; exchange rate devaluations; reduction of trade barriers; and the lifting of foreign investment barriers.[7] Designed primarily for short-run exigencies, stabilization policies focused on the immediate reduction of aggregate demand through macroeconomic management consisting of fiscal and monetary measures, and often accompanied by devaluation.[8]

Policy reform became the prerogative of the World Bank, with long-term structural transformation of the economy as its main goal. Working in conjunction with the IMF, loans were "conditional" upon the debtor countries agreeing to carry out such reforms as reducing the size of government and reducing its impact on the market place.[9]

Public Sector Capacity and Sustainability Issues

Working within a structural adjustment–induced environment, many practitioners have become aware of the demands that structural adjustment makes on public sector capability. In particular, structural adjustment programs require the state to be effective in the areas of pricing and trade policies; banking and finance; economic monitoring and data analysis; planning; and policy formulation, initiation, and implementation.[10] Such efforts at reforming public sector policies should facilitate both a strong private sector operating under market conditions and a capable, though not necessarily large, public sector committed to rational economic and social growth strategies.[11]

The generation of informed and objective information to support activity across broad areas of the economy is greatly dependent, however, upon the extent to which technical staff are insulated from legislative, interbureaucratic, and interest group pressures.[12] In sub-Saharan Africa this insulation has been difficult to accomplish, and the issue has been further complicated by what Nelson has described as a "limited analytical capacity to formulate detailed and realistic alternative approaches to adjustment."[13] As a result, both absolute shortages and the misuse or misplacement of managerial and technical personnel has also meant that critical positions are filled by expatriates.

Paradoxically, at a time when more than ever is being expected from the public sector, the resources of the state are severely limited and undermined. What this situation portends for the future has not been adequately addressed by either African governments or the international donor community. In short, rather than withering away, post–structural adjustment governments will need a strong capacity to support development activities at the national and local level, and one element of the capacity building process will require a major change in the roles of many governmental organizations and their staffs.

In the early 1980s, the political dimension of adjustment programs was clearly the weak element of the debt management strategy pursued by the international community. Despite their influence over the policy process, international organizations had little "control over the politics of adjustment inside the debtor countries."[14] Yet, as Kahler pointed out, "politics was critical in determining the bargaining behavior of debtor states."[15] Reform strategies in Africa directly confronted many vested individual and institutional interests where governments were mandated by adjustment agreements to implement policy changes. Further, opposition was as likely to come from political leadership as from public sector employees, all of whom had a stake in maintaining existing arrangements. As Nelson noted, higher-level civil servants, in particular, have favored the status quo, where many "hold extensive interests, personally or through their families, in private enterprises benefitting from existing arrangements."[16] Such opposition, coming as it does from within the state, has clearly undermined policy reform in Africa and has emphasized the need to address the politics of adjustment as well as the policies of adjustment.

The International Donor Community and Capacity Building

The factors underlying Africa's debt crisis of the 1980s and the problems that continue to plague much of the continent today are a complex blend of domestic and international behavior and influences. African governments as well as the international donor and banking community have all contributed to the present situation, either by act or omission. As many observers of the continent have noted, Africa's capacity to steer its own path, to distill development objectives, to elaborate plans and strategies, and to implement them has not developed sufficiently to meet the demands of the debt crisis. Decades of technical assistance and considerable increases in the numbers of educated and experienced Africans has not been reflected in the expansion of capacity for effective direction and control over their development.[17] The absence of adequate institutional structures to deal with external agencies as well as a "top-down" process of governance—often accompanied by a lack of transparency and accountability—have added to the alienation of African governments and their actions from the mass of the population.

Development programs around the world over the last thirty years have concentrated on the technical aspects of policy content, while the institutional aspects of good governance have been relatively neglected by all parties. Until quite recently, the institutional requirements for formulating, implementing, and maintaining policies received far less attention than the content of the policies. It appears that the basic assumptions and underlying rationale either took capacity for granted or the importance of capacity was not appreciated by the policy experts advising on and formulating policy. As a result, the standards of institutional effectiveness and efficiency in administrative and managerial capacity have been declining rather than improving in much of Africa.

Structural adjustment programs operating within this context have often had a negative impact on human resources and institutional capacity. For example, planning mechanisms have substantially broken down; the capacity to undertake policy analysis studies has not developed in line with the need for such analyses; appropriate information and statistical data bases for planning and policy formulation are scarce; serious staff recruitment and retention problems have arisen; and, finally, there is often an inability to sustain minimal budgets for operational costs. Overall, the evidence suggests that the failure to meet program goals under structural adjustment is related to administrative weakness. Many limitations of structural adjustment policies exist at the level "within bureaucracies themselves and where particular administrative structures and their environments meet."[18]

Over and above all of these debilitating factors, there is a glaring lack of institutional structures to deal effectively with external agencies. The latter have profoundly affected the capacity of developing countries, in general, to participate on an equal footing in negotiations with the international donor community. Structural adjustment programs, in particular, have been designed almost exclusively by external funding agencies. The general view has been that this situation arose not so much from a lack of capacity in Africa as from a preference on the part of the agencies to fund only programs designed by themselves. Indications of a different approach to the structural adjustment process—"structural adjustment with a human face"[19]—and the recognized need for a change in the use of technical assistance are to be welcomed. The aims should be, however, to build more confidence in Africa's capacity to design its own path and to support endogenous capacity building as a long-term process.

As a new cadre of LDC managers emerges and much of the attention once given to the public sector shifts to nongovernmental organizations (NGOs), there is a pressing need to review the lessons learned from thirty years of technical assistance. An early argument remains valid—sustainability requires institutional development. In a 1989 report, the World Bank linked the crisis in sub-Saharan Africa with sustainable growth and noted that "building private sector capacity should extend beyond helping community associations. Local nongovernmental associations can be drawn into the development effort as intermediaries. . . . Local consultants and professional associations could also be mobilized."[20]

Policymakers should define the relationship between sustainability and institutional development. Policy reform and structural adjustment provide both donors and LDCs with a second try at institutional development. Sustainability and replicability are the keys to a successful strategy for donor-supported design and implementation and an on-going assessment process for technical assistance. LDC managers are increasingly concerned to develop the capacity to insure the sustainability of project and program benefits beyond the limited time horizon of the donor's direct involvement. Increasingly, donors such as the United Nations Development Programme (UNDP), the U.S. Agency for International Development (USAID), and the World Bank have rejected the project mode[21] and see a project as a pilot for self-sustaining activity, financed by host country institutions.[22] LDC managers are more likely to see a project as an integral part of an already existing program. In both scenarios, project designers need to allow for ongoing assessment by both the donor and host country officials and to provide for the possibility of replication after the project ends. LDC program managers are painfully aware that donor-sponsored project interventions often do not yet successfully pursue these goals.[23]

One of the more successful interventions in postwar institutional development was that of the Rockefeller Foundation. Much of the foundation's efforts targeted educational and training institutions. From the beginning, the foundation focused upon selected programs with clearly defined goals. In their university development program, Rockefeller's objective was to strengthen a few universities in Africa, Asia, and Latin America and to commit significant resources over a medium range of fifteen to twenty years to ensure that a "critical mass" of technical assistance was introduced.[24] The Rockefeller experience illustrated the importance of "going first class" with a high-quality intervention of highly qualified people. The Rockefeller model of the 1970s provides important lessons for institutional development in the 1990s.

It has been twenty-five years since development scholars highlighted the role of institutional development efforts in technical assistance. Although institutions are organizationally based, the concept as used here is broader and "refers to rules, norms, and expectations that govern transactions and relations among people."[25] Organizations can be easily created, but fitting them into societal patterns is much more difficult.

Though the ideas of institutional development are not new, there is a growing realization that post–structural adjustment policies require support for institutional development.[26]

As Milton Esman and Norman Uphoff pointed out, "Governments and international donors . . . cannot confine their efforts to economic policy, infrastructural investments and technological assistance. Institutional and human resource development is also an essential component."[27] Donor intervention to improve management performance will not be suc cessful without a sustained commitment to institutional development, particularly for those institutions involved in design, implementation, education, and training. Moreover, such interventions need to be unencumbered by unrealistic time-bound constraints in the project cycle. As Jon Moris observed, the time schedules provided in donor project documents are "hopelessly unrealistic."[28] The UNDP and the World Bank have both decided to shift from project financing to program and subprogram financing so that a longer time frame can be given to the phasing of activities.

In the end, institutional development presupposes a satisfactory level of donor and/or national commitment of resources, a cadre of LDC administrators who can take control of the technical assistance program, and an institutional capacity for organizations to plan and implement human resource development activities. The failure to address these issues will necessitate the continued use of overseas facilities or the intervention by expatriate technical assistance personnel whose short-term contracts and limited vision are likely to ensure that the intervention will have a project structure rather than a program one.

Institutional Development for the Future

In the past, many of the development interventions initiated internally or with external assistance have failed to realize development objectives and promote sustainable change. A major contributing factor to these failed intervention strategies has been the absence of an adequate framework for formulating and implementing interventions. More often than not, the institutional implications of an intervention strategy have been neglected, with little or no participation from key groups or individuals having a stake in policy outcomes. In effect, a crisis of participation has developed in many countries. Having ignored and/or failed to understand the complexities of sustainable change in Africa, the essential institutional framework of structures, processes, and human resource development has been seriously mismanaged. Lingering over the landscape of scores of development-oriented programs, structural adjustment policies included, is a dark legacy: of underdeveloped and fragile institutions marginal, at best, to the policy process; of barely functioning systems of communication where information has become a scarce resource accessible to the few; and of a generation of demoralized, dispirited professionals who cannot function effectively in either the public or private sectors.

Both the historical nature of the decisionmaking process in postindependence African states and the dynamics of donor-recipient relationships have hindered the development of an institutional capacity to plan and manage change. Most African countries have tended toward a centralized machinery of government. Over the course of postindependence history, this tendency has been strengthened by the dynamics of donor relations where external agencies bypassed secondary structures in favor of relationships with central authorities. Both ideology and convenience dictated this pattern of top-down governance and created a powerful central political and administrative elite whose members often have more contact with external funding agencies than with nationals of their own countries, both inside and outside of government. Hence, a practice has evolved that is characterized by a lack of popular participation at all levels and the isolation of those involved in policymaking from the mass of the population. Misconceptions about appropriate national development strategies as well as the absence of will and legitimacy to pursue change have resulted.

Sustainable development requires a domestic capacity for the formulation and implementation of policy, a capacity that is rooted in the society, culture, and history of the country it serves. Although this capacity has long been advocated by development practitioners opposed to the top-down, blueprint approach,[29] the impetus for a second look at sustainability issues has arisen with the shift in attention away from government-managed economies to market-oriented economies. The transition process inherent in this shift of orientation, resources, power, and influence has raised many complex questions for donors and for the African governments involved.

At issue are finding workable solutions to such questions as: What is the nature and role of the state in a market-oriented economy that will maximize economic growth and development at all levels and among all sectors of the economy? What is an appropriate balance between the public and private sectors in pursuit of economic development? What constitutes appropriate levels of pluralism and decentralization that will ensure democratic participation and good governance without descending to chaos in underdeveloped societies? What are the appropriate strategies for building implementation and managerial capacity both inside and outside of government? And finally, what overall objectives can donors and African governments pursue to bring about sustainable change?

The following chapters revisit the issue of sustainable development and capacity building, employing an action research model with a focus on the dynamics of change. The approach emphasizes the practical and empirical evidence from selected African countries, especially the experiences of African researchers and practitioners resident in the countries under examination. Their analyses and recommendations address sustainable development and capacity building from the perspectives of public, non-governmental, and private organizations as well as the views of external organizations.

Capacity Building for Policy Change and Sustainability Project

The initial phase of the project culminating in this book began with a recommendation by the Development Administration Working Group of the International Institute of Administrative Sciences (IIAS) (Brussels, Belgium) for a series of case studies to be carried out in several Anglophone and Francophone countries.[30] The six countries identified by IIAS in English-speaking Africa were Ghana, Nigeria, Kenya, Tanzania, Zambia, and Botswana. In each country, the working group selected an academic and a practitioner to research and write the case studies together. The focus of the case studies was on the factors that have led to the sustainability of policy changes and on the impact that policy reform has had on capacity. Each of the research teams was asked to address the following questions during preparation of the case studies:

1. What is the nature of the policymaking/decisionmaking process in your country?
2. Does sustainability have to do with the manner in which (and the extent to which) institutional implications are taken into consideration at the formulation stage?
3. Are the designs of structures and processes of decisionmaking policy within institutions related to success or failure?
4. Are all actors who need to be involved in the process consulted? How? To what extent is consultation a prerequisite for sustainability?
5. To what extent is the problem of lack of capacity related to issues of human resource development? To what extent is it also a matter of senior decisionmakers not approaching the problem with the broadest concept of "governance" in mind?
6. How can external actors, including donors, contribute effectively to internal capacity building to introduce desired policy changes and make them sustainable?
7. To what extent is the efficiency targeted in structural adjustment programs appropriate for African states?

Because of the uniqueness of the countries involved, not all of the above questions could be answered definitively in the case studies. However, the authors did use the framework as a guide to their research. The research was carried out in 1990 and 1991, and had as its goal the identification of the political philosophy and patterns of political change required to achieve economic and social development in Africa during the 1990s.

In the next six chapters, the authors present their research findings. Chapter 2 examines Ghana, a country that observers have concluded has implemented a successful program of structural adjustment. The Ghana case study stresses the linkages between policy capacity and economic reform and the need for a strong, efficient state system. Ghana is now committed to the principles of market mechanisms. This commitment is important for both public management and public policy capacity.

Ghana initially had an advantage in terms of human resource development in the 1950s, but lost it through two decades of political instability and economic collapse. Now the country is beginning to come back economically. Political moves toward democratization have been less conclusive though the country held national elections in 1992. The country has also been strongly supported in its efforts by the world financial community, which views Ghana's reforms with favor.

In Chapter 3, the authors of the Nigeria case study reject the unfettered free-market model and argue that there must be an activist state if development management is to succeed. The mixed economy model adopted by Nigeria and other African countries at independence resulted in the dominant role of the state in the economy and in society. Initially, the availability of revenue from commodity export earnings permitted considerable progress to be made in the provision of basic infrastructure and social and welfare facilities. This initial success, however, was not sustainable because of the decline in revenue from export earnings and the lack of institutional capacity within the public sector to play a developmental role.

The failure of the public sector bureaucracy in Nigeria to measure up to the challenges of sustainable development started a movement to redefine the role of the state in national development. In this movement, policy measures were advocated to deal with the country's socioeconomic crisis and to achieve sustainable development. The policies included reform and rationalization of the civil service, the commercialization and privatization of public enterprises, and other forms of economic restructuring and stabilization.

Nigeria currently faces two related problems that hinder effective policymaking: a decisionmaking process that depends on cronyism and the purchase of political influence, and, until very recently, the unwillingness of the military regime to relinquish power to an elected civilian government. International influence on Nigeria's structural adjustment program has been limited by the country's unwillingness to accept many aspects of IMF/World Bank conditionality.

In Chapter 4, the Zambia case study stresses the importance of environmental factors on the policy process, such as the pressure for unity under the Kaunda government, the movement away from the one-party state, and the precarious nature of the Zambian economy. The authors discuss the process of government in an institutional context. There are three ways of understanding the policy process and implementation, as identified by these authors. These include:

(1) legal constraints and guidelines, (2) institutional structures and prescribed processes, and (3) individual and group behavior. The latter is particularly important.

The authors are optimistic about the move to pluralism, but caution that donor conditionality in the past resulted in urban riots. They advise that, in the future, donors should use persuasion and slower techniques and be more humane and sensitive to the impact of conditionality on society. The declaration of a state of emergency in Zambia on March 3, 1993, by President Frederick Chiluba suggests that the cautionary warnings of the authors are well taken.

In discussing capacity building in Tanzania (Chapter 5), the authors contrast the formal roles of policy institutions with their practical roles. The case study stresses the role of the constitution and the ideology of the country, and contrasts them with bureaucratic decisionmaking and modes of behavior. The authors argue that the former established rules of the game that could not be carried out. The party was to initiate policy and the government was to implement it. Under this arrangement the government ran into problems and the party leadership was shorn of power. The system did not synchronize, and the policy process was unable to meet the needs of society. In explaining what went wrong, the authors cite a lack of public involvement as the key problem. Feedback came only in the form of complaints. The failure of the one-party state eventually led to the transition to a multiparty political system in 1992.

Chapter 6 looks at the context of policymaking in Kenya. Taking an institutional approach, the author uses a broad perspective of the context and manner in which public policy formulation and implementation takes place in Kenya. Although every policymaking process is influenced by the milieu, the chapter examines three specific environmental factors: (1) the social context and the problem of ethnic considerations in "agenda setting"; (2) politics— the party, legislature, and the executive; and (3) economics. The author notes that the ruling party is peripheral and weak; that expatriates continue to have a significant role in the policymaking process; and that political parties as such have had little or no influence on the policymaking process. The author also notes several bottlenecks, especially those that adversely affect the implementation of development policies.

The political and economic crises in Kenya led to severe social and ethnic instability, and controversial multiparty elections were held in 1992. While the situation had stabilized somewhat with the completion of the elections, many of the underlying social and ethnic problems have not been addressed by the government.

The Botswana chapter (Chapter 7) offers a contrast to the other five case studies in that Botswana has never come under structural adjustment. The authors stress the country's pragmatism in policymaking and note that Botswana's population is small and that the country has no major ethnic problems. The country's political life is also dominated by the ruling Botswana Democratic Party (BDP).

Policymakers in Botswana see themselves as modernizers. Beginning at independence, the private sector has been explicitly emphasized. The role of the public sector has always been to support private sector development. Under this arrangement, policy formulation lies with the Economic Development Council, a coordinating mechanism the authors find successful. To sustain development, education and training policies have focused on both central and local government, as well as on the private sector. Human resource development remains a critical problem in the public, private, and parastatal sectors, however. The failure to address these human resource problems has the potential to undermine Botswana's capacity to carry out its development goals.

Chapter 8 presents a discussion that occurred at a workshop in Arusha, Tanzania, from June 2 to 6, 1991. Jointly organized by the IIAS and the African Association for Public Administration and Management (AAPAM) (Nairobi, Kenya), hosted by the President's Office of the United Republic of Tanzania, and co-sponsored by the Commonwealth Fund for Technical Cooperation and the Canadian International Development Agency, the workshop brought together all of the authors of the following chapters to discuss the conceptual issues arising from their research.

Four major themes dominated the discussion. First, there needs to be an appropriate balance between public sector and private sector responsibilities for social and economic development. Achieving a more proper balance will require an appropriate level of analytical capacity to develop public policies within the context of prevailing market forces and social needs.

Second, it is important for societies to be able to move from single centers of decisionmaking (usually within government) to multiple centers of decisionmaking, focusing on efforts that will decentralize government functions and promote pluralism. The decentralization of public sector decisionmaking should include both intermediate and primary units of government. Efforts to promote pluralism should include the development of multiple channels of influence and mechanisms of consultation and communication between societal associations and public sector institutions.

Third, policymakers need to find appropriate means to strengthen the implementation and management capacity in both the public and private sectors, including nongovernmental and not-for-profit agencies. A successful strategy for development will also include the identification of appropriate and market-driven development activities, which will target small-scale entrepreneurs in both urban and rural areas.

Fourth, sustainability issues are directly linked to the promotion of institutional development. The overall objective is to build capacity to design and implement policy change and to successfully manage the transition to a post–structural adjustment phase of development. Moreover, institutional development considerations must inform the activities of the private sector (both profit and not-for-profit) as well as the public sector. Development managers in all spheres must have the capacity to develop organizations and personnel appropriate for a diverse set of development-related tasks. An important requirement in the training of managers is the teaching of management techniques that emphasize an analytical or creative thinking approach to problem solving as well as emphasizing the technical aspects of developing sound policy initiatives. In the end, capacity building involves sustainable institutions, placing institutional development at the center of the development process.[31]

Chapter 9 examines institutional development within the context of human resource development—the a priori condition necessary for social and economic change. Drawing upon the experiences of four donor-supported institutional development interventions with a strong focus on human resource development, the authors assess what has worked and what has not. They found that institutional development and human resource development were more likely to occur where there was a high level of commitment among donors and host-country officials to develop collaborative models of cooperation. Collaborative arrangements may appear in many forms, but contracting-out, in particular, has several advantages. Based on a learning process model, it offers opportunities for feedback and adjustment. It also addresses important capacity building issues such as accountability and efficiency. In looking toward the future, a more concerted effort to adopt a collaborative approach to donor-supported interventions has the potential to reorder traditional donor-recipient relationships—an important but often overlooked aspect of management development strategies.

In conclusion, Chapter 10 draws on the case study experiences in an attempt to compare the findings and synthesize conclusions from the contributors to this project. At issue is the need to highlight the various factors and influences that can both hinder and help efforts to promote policy reform and sustainability in Africa. The role of the post–structural adjustment state in Africa is in the process of being redefined. Economic reform began the process of redefinition. Political and administrative reform will complete the process. To speculate about the future at this stage is inviting, but foolhardy. Only with minor certainty can we conclude that the post–structural adjustment state in Africa will be less monolithic. The forces and influences that reform efforts have set in motion will determine the outcome in each country. For the donor community and Africans in leadership positions, this is an important point for it shifts attention away from final outcomes and macrostrategies to an emphasis on building the capacity of individuals and institutions to meet the demands of change.

When emphasis was on public sector development, institutional development never got the attention it deserved, particularly among the donor community. One would hope that with the change in emphasis to private sector development and public-private partnerships this error will be corrected.

For the foreseeable future, the international donor community can be expected to maintain a significant role in the African development process. The persistent problem of debt, ongoing structural adjustment programs, and the commitment to policy reform have only reinforced the need for more donor attention to and support for institutional development activities.

The contributors to this project have offered a number of informative and realistic insights and recommendations that they hope will both interest and inform the policymakers of African governments, the international donor community, and other interested observers in Africa's pursuit of sustainable development policies.

Notes

1. See Ted Carpenter, "The New World Disorder," *Foreign Policy* (Summer 1991), pp. 24–39, and C. Fred Bergsten, "The World Economy After the Cold War," *Foreign Affairs*, vol. 69, no. 3 (Summer 1990), pp. 96–112.

2. Robert Gilpin, *The Political Economy of International Relations* (Princeton, N.J.: Princeton University Press, 1987), p. 27.

3. Milton J. Esman, *Managing Dimensions of Development Perspectives and Strategies* (Bridgeport, Conn.: Kumarian Press, 1991).

4. Joan M. Nelson, "Introduction: The Politics of Economic Adjustment in Developing Nations," in *Economic Crisis and Policy Choice: The Politics of Adjustment in the Third World*, ed. Joan M. Nelson (Princeton, N.J.: Princeton University Press, 1990), p. 12.

5. Susan George, *A Fate Worse Than Debt: The World Financial Crisis and the Poor* (New York: Grove Weidenfeld, 1988).

6. Miles Kahler, "Conclusion: Politics and Proposals for Reform," in *The Politics of International Debt*, ed. Miles Kahler (Ithaca, N.Y.: Cornell University Press, 1986), p. 258. See also Charles Lipson, "The International Organization of Third World Debt," in *Toward a Political Economy of Development: A Rational Choice Perspective*, ed. Robert H. Bates (Berkeley: University of California Press, 1988), p. 14.

7. George, *A Fate Worse than Debt*, p. 51.

8. Nelson, "Introduction," p. 4.

9. Charles Lipson, "International Debt and International Institutions," in *The Politics of International Debt*, ed. Kahler, p. 235.

10. Louis A. Picard and Michele Garrity, "Strategic Intervention and Management Effectiveness: The Program Manager's Perspective" (unpublished paper, January 15, 1992).

11. Joan M. Nelson, "Conclusions," in *Economic Crisis*, ed. Nelson, p. 347.

12. Nelson, "Introduction," p. 21.

13. Nelson, "Conclusions," p. 334.

14. Miles Kahler, "Politics and International Debt: Explaining the Crisis," in *The Politics of International Debt*, ed. Kahler, p. 31.

15. Ibid., pp. 31–32.

16. Nelson, "Conclusions," p. 357.

17. See the essays in *Economic Restructuring and African Public Administration: Issues, Actions, and Future Choices*, ed. M. Jide Balogun and Gelase Mutahaba, (Hartford, Conn.: Kumarian Press, 1989).

18. John M. Cohen, Merilee S. Grindle, and S. T. Walker, "Policy Space and Systems Research in Donor Led Rural Development," Harvard Institute for International Development *Discussion Paper* (April 1984), as quoted in Stephan Haggard, "The Politics of Adjustment: Lessons from the IMF's Extended Fund Facility," in *The Politics of International Debt*, ed. Kahler, p. 184. See also Joan Nelson, "The Political Economy of Stabilization: Commitment, Capacity, and Public Response," in *Toward a Political Economy*, ed. Bates, pp. 80–130.

19. Giovanni Andrea Cornea, Richard Jolly, and Frances Stewart, *Adjustment with a Human Face* (Oxford: Clarendon Press, 1987).

20. *Sub-Saharan Africa: From Crisis to Sustainable Growth—A Long Term Perspective Study* (Washington, D.C.: World Bank, 1989), pp. 6–7.

21. *UNDP Fifth Country Development Programme* (Addis Ababa, Ethiopia: United Nations Development Programme, n. d.), draft.

22. Louise G. White, *Creating Opportunities for Change: Approaches to Managing Development Programs* (Boulder, Colo.: Lynne Rienner Publishers, 1987), p. 6.

23. The problem is not new. In 1962, John Montgomery pointed to what he called "problems of mutuality" in donor–host country relationships. See John D. Montgomery, *The Politics of Foreign Aid: American Experience in Southeast Asia* (New York: Praeger, 1962).

24. Joseph Black, James S. Coleman, and Laurence D. Stifel, eds., *Education and Training for Public Sector Management in the Developing Countries* (New York: Rockefeller Foundation, March 1977), pp. 1–6.

25. Louise G. White, *Implementing Policy Reforms in LDCs: A Strategy for Designing and Effecting Change* (Boulder, Colo.: Lynne Rienner Publishers, 1990), p. 7.

26. White, *Implementing Policy Reforms*, pp. 6–9.

27. Milton Esman and Norman T. Uphoff, *Local Organizations: Intermediaries in Rural Development* (Ithaca, N.Y.: Cornell University Press, 1984), p. 286.

28. Jon R. Moris, *Managing Induced Rural Development* (Bloomington, Ind.: International Development Institute, 1981), p. 33.

29. See Jon R. Moris, *Managing Induced Rural Development;* Coralie Bryant and Louise G. White, *Managing Development in the Third World* (Boulder, Colo.: Westview Press, 1982); and Goran Hyden, *No Shortcuts to Progress* (Berkeley: University of California Press, 1983).

30. In early 1990, IIAS established a working group on development administration that focused on capacity building for policy change and sustainability. The group met in Brussels on June 14–15, 1990, with a follow-up meeting in Madrid on November 8–14, 1990. The working group decided to focus on enhancing capacity for development planning, policy formulation, and implementation and on the role that public-private partnerships could play in the development process. IIAS, through the working group, subsequently organized research workshops in Arusha, Tanzania, for Anglophone Africa and in Dakar, Senegal, for Francophone Africa. This book is the result of the Arusha meeting.

31. Esman, *Management Dimensions of Development.*

2

Ghana: Capacity Building for Policy Change

H. Akuoko-Frimpong

A recent study by the World Bank on sub-Saharan Africa has observed that "in the most fundamental sense, development depends on the capacity to initiate, sustain, and accommodate change."[1] The study found, however, that "weak capacity in both [the] public and private sectors is at the very core of Africa's development crisis."[2] Indeed, by the mid-1980s, the development crisis in Africa had been perceived to be a phenomenon stemming largely from weak capacity and mismanagement of economic policy at the national level. This situation was exacerbated by damaging international economic events and trends beyond the control of African governments.

To overcome the problems, African countries needed to improve day-to-day economic policymaking. Such an improvement requires "research analysis and policy advice that is country-specific; and this suggests the importance of building up policy analytic capabilities at the national level."[3] Toward this end there is "need for one or more centres of excellence on the continent."[4] At issue is the need to strengthen and enhance the sustainability of policies through a "strong sense of African ownership" of the policymaking process, which can be accomplished through "first-rate indigenous research and policy design capacity."[5]

The accumulated experiences and problems with capacity building efforts in Africa resulted in the launching of the Africa Capacity Building Initiative (ACBI) in February 1991. The main aim of the ACBI is to build and strengthen "local capacities in policy analysis and development management in sub-Saharan Africa."[6] The main sponsors of the ACBI are the World Bank, the United Nations Development Programme (UNDP), and the African Development

19

Bank. In the context of this case study, the ACBI's operational focus is significant, for it provides a convenient analytical framework for the discussion of the relevant issues on capacity building in Africa, and Ghana in particular.

The question is: What factors account for the observed problems in Africa? In this case study, an attempt was made to answer the question by a critical examination of the development strategies adopted in Ghana since the 1960s and the extent to which these strategies shaped the government's macroeconomic policies. In this regard, Ghana's efforts to achieve a balance between the public and private sectors of the economy was used to illustrate some of the problems observable in sub-Saharan economies arising from the weak capacity for policy analysis and development management.

Lessons from the Ghanaian experience were drawn largely from the country's economic policy reforms and administrative reform initiatives by governments of various political complexions since the 1960s. The highlights of these experiences are the implementation of Ghana's Economic Recovery Program (ERP) and the twin policies of ministerial restructuring and decentralization in the 1980s.

By focusing on Ghana's economic and administrative reform efforts, I attempted not only to assess the country's widely acclaimed success in the implementation of the ERP but also to critically examine the program for the decentralization of government and the restructuring of ministerial organizations. Through restructuring, the government sought to strengthen the policy coordination capacities that had weakened over the years.[7] The decentralization policy focused on restructuring institutions and processes that would enhance the participation of people at all levels of administration, bringing about greater efficiency and productivity in government.[8]

Under the adopted analytical framework, the pertinent issues addressed in the case study included the following: the nature of high-level decisionmaking and the policy process; the relationship between the design of structures and processes of decisionmaking within institutions, and the success or failure of past policy; the institutional implications for policy change and sustainability; the impact of consultation on sustainability of policy change; the problem of inadequate capacity and human resource development; and the role of external actors in internal capacity building for policy change and sustainability.

The case study also demonstrated the significance of the following view:

African governments and the international donor community have all contributed to the present [crisis in Africa] either by act or omission. There has been a relative neglect of the institutional aspects of good governance by all parties. The development programmes [of African countries] of the last thirty years concentrated on technical aspects of policy content. The institutional requirements for formulating, implementing and maintaining these policies did not get the same attention as policy content. Either the capacity was taken for granted or its importance was not appreciated by the policy experts advising on and formulating policy.[9]

The significance of this observed phenomenon in Africa will become apparent from a critical analysis of Ghana's experience in capacity building for policy change and sustainability since the 1960s.

The Economic Policy Framework

In Ghana the available evidence shows "the extent to which the economic policy framework of each government that has emerged . . . over the past three decades has shaped the development of both the public and private sectors of the economy and as a result, determined the level of their contribution toward the country's social and economic development."[10]

For instance, the economic policies of the government during the 1950s attempted to promote the development of both the public and private sectors of the economy. This effort occurred during a period when high-level decisionmaking and the policy process depended to a large extent on the technical inputs from a relatively efficient and effective (albeit less development-oriented) bureaucracy bequeathed by the British colonial administration. At that time Ghana's capacity for policy change and sustainability was manifested not only by the quality of the policy content but also by the efficiency of the structures and processes of policy-level decisionmaking, implementation, and maintenance that had been created under the tutelage of technocrats of high caliber.

The gradual buildup of capacity in Ghana in the late 1950s continued into the early 1960s. But from the mid-1960s the relative strength of the bureaucracy in policy analysis and development management was put to a severe test. These years found the Ghanaian environment increasingly characterized by political and economic instability, which had the effect of not only reducing Ghanaian ownership of policy sustainability but also marginalizing the value of indigenous institutional requirements for formulating, implementing, and maintaining policies. The changes in development strategy included the centralization of decisionmaking and the departure of the remaining colonial technocrats within the bureaucracy. The latter were replaced by increasing government dependence on foreign scholars and experts for economic policy advice. The significance of the period was underlined by the idea that the government of Kwame Nkrumah "broke out of the 'colonial' mould and switched decisively to a socialist strategy. The strategy rejected an open, market-oriented economy and instituted a planned, regulated and centralized economy in which the state was to become the predominant economic agent and the pursuit of development was to be given priority."[11]

It is important to note, however, that the government's development strategy during the 1950s and 1960s was not determined primarily by ideology but rather by pragmatism. For instance, in the 1950s President Nkrumah's government had always taken the view that the number of publicly owned commercial enterprises that had been set up under the umbrella of the Industrial Development Corporation (established in 1951) should be privatized or sold to private entrepreneurs when they had become viable.[12] As late as 1958, the government established a committee to explore ways of assisting Ghanaian entrepreneurs.

However, Nkrumah became increasingly disillusioned with the local private sector and eventually came to believe that there was "little realistic prospect of fostering an indigenous [private] entrepreneurial class capable of industrialising the country at the speed he wanted."[13] In 1960 came the announcement that development efforts would focus on cooperatives rather than privately owned enterprises, that state-owned enterprises (SOEs) would remain publicly owned, and that private enterprise would no longer receive special assistance.[14]

The weak capacity of Ghanaian private entrepreneurs to respond positively to the government's economic policies did not, however, weaken the government's confidence in the role of private enterprise in the country's socioeconomic development process. Rather, the government adopted a pragmatic approach by looking beyond Ghanaian entrepreneurs. This approach was clearly demonstrated in the government's 1965 Annual Plan, which confidently stated that "the policy of encouraging foreign private investors will be prosecuted with increased vigour."[15]

Nkrumah's support for local private enterprise declined in the early 1960s, but he continued to support foreign direct investment, pointing out that "it brought in much-needed managerial and technical skills which could be passed on to Ghanaians."[16] Consequently, when the Capital Investment Act of 1963 was passed, it offered "a wide range of fiscal and other concessions to would-be [foreign] investors."[17]

Within the unfolding development strategy of the government, there were many strings attached to foreign investment. Clearly, the strategy was to structure foreign investment in ways that allowed the state to maintain control over domestic economic activity.[18] Public enterprises and a mixed economy were to become the vehicles for development. The policy underlined a marked shift in the government's development strategy from private sector to public sector development. The question at this point is: Why did the economic policies of the government fail to make the desired positive and sustainable impact on the growth of Ghana's economy? Was it due to weak capacity for policy change and sustainability in the economy at that time?

It can be argued that Ghana's bureaucracy in the early 1960s had the capacity to offer policy advice of high quality. This capacity was demonstrated by the work of Ghanaian technocrats at the Planning Commission and the Bank of Ghana. In addition, the government sought and used the advice of prominent foreign economists.[19] More significantly, Ghana's 1963 Seven-Year Development Plan had substantial policy inputs from both Ghanaian technocrats and foreign scholars. Hence the view that what Nkrumah was trying to do in the 1960s "was in consonance with the ideas of most [foreign] development economists."[20] Given the quality of the content of the government's macroeconomic policies at that time and the support provided by foreign scholars in internal capacity building efforts, it could be further argued that the failure of the government's economic policies to make the desired positive and sustainable impact on the growth of the economy stemmed from the marginalization of consultation as a prerequisite for sustainability. Further, it could be argued that policy failures resulted from neglect of the institutional requirements for policy formulation, implementation, and maintenance, rather than from lack of policy analysis capabilities at the national level. In the latter case, it is noteworthy that most of the Ghanaian technocrats of proven policy analysis capability who helped to shape the economic policies of Nkrumah's government in the early 1960s were retained by subsequent governments in the late 1960s and early 1970s.[21]

Some have concluded that after the overthrow of Nkrumah's government in February 1966, the military regime of the National Liberation Council (NLC) (1966–1969) and the civilian regime of the Progress Party (PP) (1969–1972) returned to a more decentralized, market-oriented economy; and that after 1972, when it appeared that a market approach had failed, the second military government (National Redemption Council [NRC]/Supreme Military Council [SMC] of 1972–1979) again returned to a command economy.[22]

The reality was that "continuity rather than change was the outstanding characteristic of policies from 1966 onwards."[23] Although policies regarding public enterprises, foreign companies, the promotion of small and medium-sized indigenous enterprises, and foreign investment changed during this time,[24] the significance of the changes related more to implementation and sustainability factors than to policy content or orientation. In particular, these policies were adapted so that more efforts would be directed at enhancing consultation, public education, and institutional development.[25] In fact, during this period "more emphasis was put on the role of the private enterprise, and on the need for efficiency in the [SOEs] sector, less importance was attached to non-commercial objectives, and some state enterprises were returned to the private sector."[26] This period also marked the beginning of privatization in Ghana.[27]

The economic policies pursued by the NRC/SMC (1972–1979) also sought to strengthen the private sector's contribution to Ghana's social and economic development. Nonetheless, a marked increase in the role of the state as an entrepreneur was also observable. The state demonstrated increased participation in the economy when it acquired a 55 percent share in a number of foreign-owned companies in several sectors of the economy—an act that seemed to support one of the conditions attached to Nkrumah's policy on participation of foreign interests in the economy. In consonance with Ghana's sustained policy of promoting a better balance between the public and private sectors of the economy, the NRC/SMC government enunciated policies aimed at "healthy competition between the public and private enterprises."[28] Although the government's role was maintained in creating an enabling environment "which could stimulate individual initiative and private enterprise," the government also reserved the right "to intervene directly in production to stimulate rapid economic development."[29]

The NRC/SMC government recognized that the private sector was capable of playing a vital role in Ghana's socioeconomic development efforts. As a result, during the 1975/76–1979/80 Five-Year Development Plan period, the government not only expected the role of the private sector to "increase to a much faster pace so that its contribution to both national output and employment [would] be greater" but also sought to "strengthen the facilities offered by various institutions set up to aid private investors in the economy."[30]

Weakened capacity building for policy change and sustainability undermined some of the economic policies of the regimes that emerged in the country in the late 1960s and the early 1970s. The capacity of the central bureaucracy for policy analysis and economic management was clearly stretched, following a decade of political and economic instability. Indeed, by the late 1970s the problem of weak institutional capacity (including human resource development) had to be addressed as a marked decline in the economy became apparent. Further, as the economy worsened, many skilled professionals left the country.[31] The loss of capable professionals in all sectors of the economy inevitably undermined the country's efforts at capacity building.

The development of an internal capacity for policy analysis and development management suffered accordingly. In particular, the research capacity of the country's universities and research institutions markedly declined, largely caused by the exodus of senior members of staff from the country and inadequate funds for research. For instance, by the mid-1970s the Department of Economics at the University of Ghana, Legon, "had built up substantial research and training capacity on the strength of about 85 percent of its full staff establishment at post: but by the early 1980s the staff strength at the Department was as low as 21 percent."[32]

Although the unfolding economic policies of the NRC/SMC government were largely maintained by the succeeding civilian People's National Party (PNP) government,[33] finding appropriate solutions to the problems in the economy remained elusive until the emergence of the Provisional National Defence Council (PNDC) government on December 31, 1981. The PNP government had succeeded in enacting the Investment Code of 1981, designed "to open up the economy to uninhibited foreign investment and to guarantee the investor the [necessary] incentives."[34] This document provided the economic policy framework for the enactment of the PNDC government's Investment Code of 1985, which has made a significant and positive impact on Ghana's efforts at rebalancing the public and private sectors of the economy.[35] The extent to which the PNDC government has coped with the problem of capacity building for economic policy change and sustainability in the 1980s and early 1990s is described below.

Capacity in Policy Analysis
and Development Management

As noted, Ghana's declining economy and the unstable political environment had a negative impact on institutional and human resource development. Ghana's experiences were indicative of conditions in many sub-Saharan countries at the time. A World Bank document noted that "too often in Africa critical public policy issues are inadequately analysed; little relevant and timely research is done by African universities and other centres of policy research; Africa data sources are generally inadequate or unreliable; and high level African officials in key economic ministries are sometimes poorly trained and equipped."[36]

The World Bank faulted both political and economic factors for the poor state of policy analysis and management development. In the bank's view, the unfavorable political conditions had not "been conducive to the growth or sustenance of independent human or institutional capacity" and had lowered demand for policy analysis and advice, weakened morale in government ministries, and led to the neglect of educational and research institutions.[37] The financial crisis compounded the problem as deficit reduction policies led to budget cuts throughout the public sector "resulting in serious shortages of funds for research, training, institution building and education in general."[38] The bank also acknowledged a lack of surprise that expatriates were increasingly being substituted for African managers and administrators, given current conditions. The bank report concluded that such "stop-gap" measures were not the long-term solution to the problem. Rather, it noted that in the long run "there is no substitute for Africa having its own indigenous capacity."[39]

Few developing countries had suffered such rapid economic decline between the early 1970s and the early 1980s as Ghana. During the decade Ghana's real GDP "remained almost stagnant with per capita incomes declining at an annual rate of 3.1 per cent."[40] Inflation also accelerated rapidly with rates of 100 percent common, and the consumer price index increased at an average of 80 percent per annum from 1975, reaching triple digits in 1981. The rate of acceleration was one of the highest among developing countries.[41]

More significantly, the large reservoir of skilled and trained manpower that characterized Ghana in the late 1960s had been markedly reduced by the early 1980s as a result of a "tremendous exodus" of managerial and professional personnel to other countries with relatively better living conditions.[42] This exodus had a negative impact on Ghana's efforts at capacity building. By the end of the 1980s, however, Ghana's remarkable success with the management of ERP I and II on a sustainable basis was an outcome of the country's enhanced capacity for policy analysis and development management. In large measure the support provided by both bilateral and multilateral donor agencies contributed immensely to Ghana's efforts at internal capacity building in several sectors of the economy.

Institutional and human resource development capacity was to be strengthened in a number of ways during both the first and second phase of the ERP and were mainly targeted at financial reforms, improving the management of publicly owned enterprises, and civil service reforms.

Since mid-1987 the government has been implementing a comprehensive restructuring of the financial sector directed at strengthening financial institutions and enhancing their effectiveness. In addition to the implementation of new banking and finance-related laws and regulations, a major effort to improve the management performance of banks has been undertaken. These improvements have included changes in the banks' boards of directors and other senior management positions of the banks as well as the introduction of new accounting standards and audit guidelines. To facilitate local decisionmaking the Ghana Association of Bankers is collaborating with the Central Bank of Malaysia to establish a central credit data base. To upgrade the skills of the finance sector, efforts are being made to develop professional training programs for both bankers and accountants through the formation of a banking college. Finally, preparatory work is now underway to mount a second phase of financial reforms that will, among other things, strengthen both the institutional and operational effectiveness of the Bank of Ghana, enhance the effectiveness of nonfinancial institutions, and continue the training of bankers and accountants.[43]

Ghana's experience with financial sector reforms clearly demonstrates the gradual enhancement of the country's capacity for policy analysis and development management. The financial reforms have been relatively smooth, but the reform of the state enterprise sector has been less successful, indicating that the focus of reform efforts has been on policy content at the expense of the institutional requirements necessary for policy change and sustainability. In part, the nature and scope of SOEs has presented formidable problems to effecting quick solutions in this sector.[44] Although considerable attention has been given to improving management and efficiency through staffing reductions, training programs, management information systems, and support for the preparation of plans, budgets, and audit documents, major concerns remain about the performance of the sector.[45]

Civil service reforms have included a phased reduction in its size, the recruitment of skilled Ghanaians to strengthen policy planning coordination in the higher levels of government, and the provision of logistical support to agencies responsible for implementing the recovery program.[46]

The reform efforts in the SOE sector have clearly demonstrated the need to take institutional implications into consideration at the policy formulation stage. Despite the recurring problems of SOEs, the reforms here and in the financial sector have demonstrated Ghana's improved capacity for policy analysis and development management. The country's remarkable success with the ERP to date underlines Ghana's inherent potential for capacity building, albeit with the collaboration and assistance of the donor community. We now turn to Ghana's experiences with administrative reform.

Administrative Reform Efforts

The decade following the demise of the First Republic (1960–1966) in Ghana was critical in the country's political and administrative transformation. The decade was one of political instability, as well as governmental efforts to restructure the machinery of government at the subnational level on a more rational basis. In the latter case, the adoption of an integrated system of government and administration in the Ghanaian political system in the early 1970s remains highly significant. Under this system of decentralized administration, there is only one integrated organization for government and administration provided at each regional and district level, and it is composed of central government officials and local representatives.[47]

This system of decentralized administration has been accepted in principle by regimes of various political complexions since the late 1960s. Thus, for over two decades there has been a consensus on the system of decentralized administration best suited to the Ghanaian situation. Nonetheless, Ghana's experience with the implementation of the decentralization policy has so far been disappointing.[48]

During the decade following the demise of the Third Republic (1979–1981) the PNDC government also introduced innovative measures to ensure popular participation in the decisionmaking process and began a fundamental restructuring of ministerial organizations. In particular, the latter measure was designed to restore to the ministries the "policy coordination capacities which they have lost over the years, and shed them of any responsibilities for the implementation of national development programmes."[49]

Whereas the policy of promoting participatory democracy in the Ghanaian political subsystem has made an appreciable impact, the program for restructuring ministerial organizations has not yet yielded the desired outcomes.

What factors account for Ghana's relatively low achievement rate with regard to administrative reform efforts? It could be argued that an inherently weak institutional capacity to accommodate policy changes designed to ensure administrative efficiency has been a major factor. This weakness is demonstrated by the inability of most of the relevant ministries and departments to respond positively to the requirements of the ministerial restructuring and decentralization policies.

For instance, the implementation of the decentralization policy has been ongoing since 1974, yet a considerable number of ministries and departments have not decentralized their operations. Delays and inaction remain the norm despite the efforts of the Public Administration Restructuring and Decentralisation Implementation Committee (PARDIC) since the latter part of 1982 to explain the rationale behind the restructuring of ministries. The less than enthusiastic response to the latest reform efforts can be detected in similar administrative reform initiatives going back to the 1950s. The success rate of such initiatives has always been relatively low.

Decentralization and Ministerial Restructuring

Political Will and Policy Implementation

It is generally recognized that decentralization has been one of the major policies adopted by successive governments in Ghana since the late 1960s. However, the reality of the political and administrative culture in Ghana has stalled real progress of the policy. The lack of political will and the unwillingness of those entrusted with power at the national level to delegate authority to subnational units of government have had an impact on the successful implementation of the policy.[50]

Indeed, with the exception of the PNDC government, the aims and objectives of the decentralization policy as set forth by the administrative reformers of the late 1960s have been interpreted in varying degrees to serve the purposes of different regimes.[51] Excluding the PNDC government, none of the past regimes has seriously addressed the issues of effective implementation of the policy. Although the NRC/SMC government (1972–1979)

attempted to address the issue by setting up the Okoh Commission (1974–1976), the subsequent preoccupation with the search for a viable national government (under what was described as union government) effectively relegated decentralization to a low priority.

The relatively low priority accorded to decentralization in the late 1970s continued until the assumption of power by the PNDC on December 31, 1981. The PNDC regime exhibited both political will and a sense of confidence within the higher levels of political leadership about genuinely transferring power and the required resources to lower levels of government. It is clear that under the PNDC government an essential prerequisite for effective implementation appears to have been satisfied, allowing decentralization to go forward.[52]

The Ghanaian experience highlights not only the institutional implications of policy change and sustainability but also the need for governments to have the will to approach policy issues in a manner that takes into full account the overall interest of the governed. Ghana's experience under the PNDC has been encouraging.

Participation and Policy Implementation

Despite real constraints in the administration reform process (shortages of personnel and funds and relatively low levels of commitment), it can be argued that the PNDC commitment to the decentralization policy has made it possible to expand popular participation in the governance of the country. The success of the district assembly concept is illustrative. The creation of 110 district, municipal, and metropolitan assemblies by the PNDC government has made it possible for elected and appointed assembly members to work with ministry and department officials in the promotion of social and economic development. The new system seeks to ensure both the effective and efficient management of the development process in the country. It has been recognized that more work needs to be done to ensure the full realization of the aims and objectives of the government's twin policy of decentralization and ministerial restructuring, but the opening up of the policy process has been a significant step forward.

Strengthening Domestic Capacity

Unlike Ghana's experience with economic reforms, the policies that have shaped the process of administrative reform in recent years have largely been the work of indigenous technocrats, experts, and politicians.[53] There is a need, however, for the government to maintain the momentum generated for capacity building. Toward this end, the establishment of the national Policy Analysis and Coordination Center (PACC) is desirable. As a research and intelligence organization, PACC will be expected to coordinate the efforts of the various bodies in the country that have an impact on capacity building, thereby creating a more rational framework for policy analysis and development management. This initiative, however, needs to be accompanied by efforts to strengthen the country's universities, research bodies, and management development institutions to enable them to contribute more toward human resource development.

Conclusion

The Ghana case study has revealed a number of factors that have contributed to a gradual and potentially sustainable process of capacity building. First, pragmatism rather than a dominant ideology has influenced economic policies and reform efforts. Second, a weakening economy and political instability hindered capacity building initiatives, as a mass exodus of professional and managerial talent left the country and funding for research activity and higher educational institutions decreased. The success of the Economic Recovery Program, however, with its emphasis on upgrading management skills in the banking and state enterprise sector, has begun to improve management performance in Ghana. Third, civil service reforms and administrative reform have also begun to show results. In particular, the program for ministerial reorganization and efforts to decentralize have increased popular participation in the policy process and have highlighted the importance of political will as a significant factor in transforming the public sector and enhancing capacity. Much more needs to be done in Ghana, particularly in the development of participatory governmental institutions. The donor community continues to play a significant role in macroeconomic policymaking. Increasingly, the policy process in Ghana is evolving toward Ghanaian ownership through policies that promote both institutional and human resource development. Policy successes such as the ERP indicate that sustainability factors are being addressed through more focused attention on developing indigenous capacity.

Notes

1. The World Bank, *Sub-Saharan Africa: From Crisis to Sustainable Growth, A Long-Term Perspective Study* (Washington, D.C.: The International Bank for Reconstruction and Development, 1989), p. 38.
2. Ibid.
3. Catherine Gwin, *Rockefeller Foundation Meeting on Capacity Building in International Economics in Africa: Summary of Discussion* (New York: Rockefeller Foundation, July 22–23, 1985), p. 3.
4. Ibid.
5. The World Bank, *The African Capacity Building Initiative: Toward Improved Policy Analysis and Development Management* (Washington, D.C.: The International Bank for Reconstruction and Development, 1991), p. 5.
6. Ibid., p. 1.
7. See *Report of the Public Administration Restructuring and Decentralisation Implementation Committee (PARDIC)* (Accra, Ghana: Government Printer, 1990).
8. See Preamble to PNDC (Establishment) Proclamation of 1981.
9. See Louis A. Picard with V. Moharir and J. Corkery, "Capacity Building for Policy Change and Sustainability: Lessons from the African Experience" (paper delivered to the Development Administration Working Group, IIAS, Brussels, Belgium, October 1990).
10. H. Akuoko-Frimpong, *Rebalancing the Public and Private Sectors in Developing Countries: The Case of Ghana* (Paris: OECD Development Centre Technical Papers, no. 14, June 1990), p. 18.
11. Tony Killick, *Development Economics in Action: A Study of Economic Policies in Ghana* (London: Heinemann, 1978), p. 229.
12. See ibid., p. 36.
13. Ibid., p. 37.
14. Ibid., pp. 36–37. Also see *Ghanaian Times* (Accra), October 10, 1960.
15. See Republic of Ghana, *Annual Plan for the Second Plan Year (of the 1963 Seven–Year Development Plan)* (Accra: Ministry of Information and Broadcasting, 1965). Cited in H. Akuoko-Frimpong, *Rebalancing the Sectors,* p. 18. Also see K. B. Asante, "Privatisation of Public Enterprises: The Case of Ghana," in African Association for Public Administration and Management (AAPAM), *Public Enterprise Performance and Privatisation Debate: A Review of the Options for Africa* (New Delhi: Vikas Publishing House PVT Ltd, 1987), p. 420.
16. Killick, *Development Economics,* p. 37.
17. Ibid.
18. In the words of Nkrumah: "The Government accepts the operation in the country of large-scale enterprises by foreign interests, provided that they accept the following conditions: first, that foreign private enterprises give the Government the first option to buy their shares, whenever it is intended to sell all or part of the equity capital; and secondly, that foreign private enterprises and enterprises jointly owned by the state and foreign interests be required to re-invest 60 percent of their net profits in Ghana." In addition, Nkrumah stated: "The domestic policy of (the) government is the complete ownership of the economy by the state." See ibid., pp. 37–38.
19. Including W. Arthur Lewis, Dudley Seers, and Nicholas Kaldor.
20. Killick, *Development Economics,* p. 53.
21. In particular, E. N. Omaboe and J. H. Mensah played significant roles in shaping the economic policies of the government during the period.

22. Killick, *Development Economics*, pp. 299–300.

23. Akuoko-Frimpong, *Rebalancing the Sectors*, p. 19.

24. Ibid.; Killick, *Development Economics*, p. 300.

25. For example, policy continuity is evident in the relative success of the policy of promoting indigenous private entrepreneurship in the economy—a policy that has, indeed, been maintained by all subsequent regimes of various political complexions. The policy emanated from the NLC government's Ghanaian Enterprises Decree of 1968, the PP government's Aliens' Compliance Order of 1969, and the Business Promotion Act (334) of 1970.

26. See International Bank for Reconstruction and Development (IBRD), *Study of Public Enterprises in Ghana: Final Report*, vol. 1, no. 4 (November 1985), p. 82.

27. H. Akuoko-Frimpong, "The State as an Entrepreneur in Ghana: An Analysis of the Challenge Posed by Private Entrepreneurship," in ibid., vol. 8, no. 4 (December 1988), p. 319.

28. K. B. Asante, "Privatisation," p. 429.

29. Ibid.

30. See Republic of Ghana, *Five-Year Development Plan (1975/76–1979/80)*, part 1 (Accra: Ministry of Economic Planning, January 1977), p. 43. Cited in Akuoko-Frimpong, *Rebalancing the Sectors*, p. 20.

These institutions included the Bank of Ghana, National Investment Bank, Agricultural Development Bank, Capital Investment Board (now National Investment Centre), and the Office of Business Promotion. The latter was subsequently transformed into the Ghanaian Enterprises Development Commission, and then merged with the National Board for Small-Scale Industries in January 1991. The National Board for Small-Scale Industries had been set up in 1985 to coordinate the promotion of entrepreneurship development in the Ghanaian economy. In addition, institutional support was provided by the Management Development and Productivity Institute (MDPI) through its Ghanaian Business Bureau (now transformed into Private Sector Development Management).

31. The World Bank, *Ghana: Policies and Programme for Adjustment* (Washington D.C.: The World Bank, 1984), p. xv. The World Bank report in reviewing this period noted that it was characterized, in varying intensity, by persistent high inflation, declining production and exports, flourishing illegal activities (including "kalabule"), and political instability. The report further noted that a gradual decline in per capita income had also increased the incidence of absolute poverty and that this increase was accompanied by a worsening of income distribution and growing unemployment.

32. H. Akuoko-Frimpong, *Report on a Survey of Advanced Research and Training Capacity in International Economics at African Universities and Other Institutions* (New York: Rockefeller Foundation, February 1986), p. 28. Report prepared at the request of the International Relations Division of the Rockefeller Foundation.

33. The People's National Party government followed a brief but significant intervention in government by the Armed Forces Revolution Council (AFRC) from June 4 to September 24, 1979.

34. See Republic of Ghana, *Two Years of Rehabilitation and Redirection (24th September 1979–24th September 1981)* (Accra: Ministry of Information and Tourism, September 1981), p. 1.

35. See Akuoko-Frimpong, *Rebalancing the Sectors*.

36. The World Bank, *African Capacity*, p. 7.

37. Ibid., p. 10.
38. Ibid., pp. 10–11.
39. Ibid., p. 7.
40. The World Bank, *Ghana,* p. 1.
41. Ibid.
42. Ibid.
43. For a more detailed discussion of these reforms, see Republic of Ghana, *Enhancing the Human Impact of the Adjustment Programme, Report Prepared by the Government of Ghana for the Sixth Meeting of the Consultative Group for Ghana* (otherwise known as Donors' Conference), Paris, May 14–15, 1991 (Accra: Tema Press of the Ghana Publishing Corporation, April 1991), p. 1.
44. The latest available evidence shows that the SOE sector presently includes more than 340 enterprises, statutory boards, authorities, and corporations. SOEs are dominant in the mining, energy, utilities, business, and financial services sectors of the total economy; and, in the modern formal sector SOEs are predominant in construction, transportation, and communications, as well as in wholesale and retail trade. At the census of 1984 more than 240,000 workers were employed in public enterprises, of which nearly 60,000 were employed at the Ghana Cocoa Board and its subsidiaries. See ibid.
45. For a comprehensive account of the problems of and reform efforts in this sector, see William A. Adda, PNDC secretary (minister) and chairman of the State Enterprises Commission, "The Role of the State: Restructuring Public Enterprises" (paper presented at the Senior Policy Seminar on the Impact of Industrial Policy Reforms: Public and Private Enterprise Experiences, organized jointly by the Economic Development Institute of the World Bank and the Ghana Institute of Management and Public Administration [GIMPA], Greenhill, Achimota, Accra, March 21–27, 1991); IBRD, *Public Enterprises,* vol. 1, no. 4, p. 95; and Akuoko-Frimpong, *Rebalancing the Sectors,* p. 24.
46. See a summary of an address by Dr. Kwesi Botchwey, PNDC secretary (minister) for the Ministry of Finance and Economic Planning at the First National Seminar on Private Sector Development in Ghana (Accra, April 15, 1988) organized by the United Nations Development Programme (UNDP), Accra. Summary given in Akuoko-Frimpong, *Rebalancing the Sectors,* p. 13.
47. See also H. Akuoko-Frimpong, "Decentralized Administration: The Ghanaian Experience," in Commonwealth Secretariat, *Decentralized Administration in Africa: Policies and Training Experience* (London: Management Development and Programme, Commonwealth Secretariat, 1989), p. 155.
48. Ibid.
49. *Report of PARDIC* (see Note 7).
50. For example, see H. Akuoko-Frimpong, "Decentralized Administration," p. 160. For the sake of political expediency, the Progress Party (PP) government (1969–1972) could not implement the decentralization policy without severe modifications of its aims and objectives.
51. Both decentralization and ministerial restructuring had as their goals the following: to promote efficiency and effectiveness in the management of the public services; to change the existing content of work of most public officers by distinguishing the policy planning and coordinating roles of the ministry head office from the implementing or operational roles of the departments and the districts; to ensure increased

management competence in the implementation of public decisions closest to the area of implementation in a decentralized organization; to discourage and even to prevent ministerial organizations from involvement in day-to-day management of government departments and the management of the smallest projects in the district locations; and, more significantly, to restrict ministerial organizations to policy planning coordination. In addition, the decentralization policy is expected to achieve a fundamental restructuring of the machinery of government, introducing more democratic forms of participation and greater efficiency and productivity in the state machinery.

52. Akuoka-Frimpong, "Decentralized Administration," pp. 160–163.

53. The success of the current search by the PNDC government for a viable framework for constitutional government in the country is further testimony to Ghana's improved capacity to effect sustainable policy changes.

It must also be acknowledged that the contributions of the donor community, including the UNDP, the World Bank, and the British Overseas Development Administration in particular, continue to be important in efforts to improve and strengthen domestic capacity.

3

Nigeria: Civil Service Reform and Development

Ali D. Yahaya & Ason Bur

Africa is engulfed in a social and economic crisis of immense proportions. The crisis can be partly attributed to the failure of the state to achieve the objectives of national security, socioeconomic development, and national development goals.[1] This chapter examines Nigeria's experience with capacity building for policy change and argues that successful development policies must address the question of state failure.

Development Policy and the State

The state in Africa, as in other Third World countries, exercises a dominant role in national development and has been historically conditioned. The failure of the market to promote economic growth during the colonial period led to the acceptance of the Keynesian macroeconomic model as a policy option. First in Europe and subsequently in Third World countries, Keynesian theory became the intellectual rationale for state intervention in the economy. The dominance and logic of state intervention in the economy inevitably led to the leading role of the state in politics and society, as the contemporary modern welfare state assumed economic and social responsibility on behalf of the people. As the state assumed control of the commanding heights of the economy and took center stage in national development, this action had implications for the civil service, expanding both its size and scope. As government attempted to implement an array of development-oriented programs, it increasingly strengthened and localized the bureaucracy with the unintended consequences of creating an inefficient and oversized state.

Nigeria's progress in the provision of social and welfare facilities was significant during the 1950s and in the period immediately after independence and precipitated an immense optimism and high expectation among the people. This was an era of buoyant revenue derived from the world prices for Nigerian commodities. Resources were readily available to government, and these were expended heavily in the provision of basic infrastructure and education.

Unfortunately, Nigeria's initial successes were not sustainable, and optimism soon gave way to disillusionment and political crisis as the country collapsed into civil war and was governed by successive military regimes.[2] The capacity of the state to meet the social demands placed upon it rapidly diminished. Public sector performance became increasingly less effective and efficient, leading to the present social and economic crisis confronting Nigeria. In the process the bureaucracy came to exert a disproportionate influence on policymaking.

Paradoxically, the dominance of the Nigerian state in the economy and society has been the basis of its greatest weakness. The expansion and scope of the contemporary Nigerian state without complementary efforts to build institutional capacity and a viable political process has undermined the state as an instrument of development and made sustainable development impossible.

Redefining the Role of the State

The failure of many African states to become an instrument of development has unleashed a movement for a redefinition of the role of the state in the pursuit of national social and economic goals. As the movement has gained momentum it has focused on the contemporary crisis of the modern state in Africa, and there is increasing demand that the African state should be relieved of a number of functions. Both the private sector and nongovernmental organizations (NGOs) are being called upon to assume larger roles in development efforts. In Nigeria such concerns have resulted in policies directed at reform of the civil service, the privatization of public enterprises, and the disengagement of the state from the provision of most goods and services.

Redefining the state should not be confused with dismantling the state. It simply means a recasting or a reformulation of development objectives and policy instruments and of the ways in which the state can best facilitate economic growth and development. Just how far the state should retreat from its previous level of involvement, however, remains a source of controversy. As one European observer has noted:

Africa needs the support of states to extricate itself from the current situation and to encourage its own development. Let us help the states to act in another manner, let us not [deprive] them of their essential responsibility. Let us not apply our criteria—albeit even sometimes contested in the developed countries—to those countries which are in a pre-economy state. Let them invent a development model and process; but there is no development without a state.[3]

From the above, it is obvious that the state will continue to be actively involved in the development of African economies. In particular, the state must have a role in building capacity for economic policy formulation and implementation.

Policy Reform in Nigeria

One major action undertaken in Nigeria to resolve the present economic crisis is a structural adjustment program. A number of policy elements constitute the economic recovery program including: the strengthening of demand management policies; the adoption of measures to stimulate domestic production and broaden the supply base of the economy; changes in the exchange rate policy and restructuring of the tariff regime; trade liberalization and the reduction of administrative controls; the adoption of more appropriate pricing policies; and the rationalization and commercialization and, in some cases, the privatization of public enterprises.

These decisions have imposed new demands on the state and require more effective and efficient performance from the public sector. The challenges facing the public sector under this program are inevitably more complex; consequently, management capacity under the program must be of high quality in order to enhance performance. Given the latter, the need for capacity building has been recognized in Nigeria, and a systematic and structured strategy has been adopted toward this end, involving stakeholders, beneficiaries, interest groups, and public officers and political leaders.

The Policy Analysis Framework in Nigeria

Public policy in Nigeria is the end product of a series of activities and decisions carried out at different stages and at different government levels, each of which is important in its own right and includes key institutional, group, and individual participants. Thus, public policy is not only influenced by special interest groups; it is also affected by the three tiers of government at which policies are made, articulated, and implemented.

Nigeria is a federation of twenty-one states and the federal capital territory of Abuja. The states are subdivided into 504 local government areas. Each of the three levels of government (federal, state, and local) makes public policies. Similar to the activities of special interest groups, these competing government authorities represent distinct ideas about how social authority and responsibility should be allocated. Although military control of the present government has given a false sense of federally led public policies that work harmoniously at each level of authority, the political structure of the country ensures competing interests among the three tiers of government.

There are three organs of government that have responsibility for policymaking under the federal military government. The most important and highest is the Armed Forces Ruling Council (AFRC). It comprises approximately nineteen members drawn from key sections of the armed forces and is headed by the president of Nigeria and the commander in chief of the armed forces. The inspector general of police is also a member. In the main, the AFRC combines the role of the legislature, the executive, and the judiciary (in dispensing the prerogative of mercy). The situation is informed by the nature of the military, which is a highly centralized bureaucracy.

The second body is the National Council of States, which comprises all the state military governors, the service chiefs, and the president, who chairs the council meetings. The council addresses national issues such as the national budget, national development plans, and other matters having state implications.

Third, there is the Federal Executive Council (FEC), or Council of Ministers. FEC meetings are presided over by the president. The FEC is the executive arm of the military government. In most cases it initiates policy matters and also ensures their faithful implementation. Both military and civilian ministers are members of the FEC. In the main, the AFRC, the Council of States, and the FEC are the policymaking organs under the federal military government of Nigeria.

At the state level, the State Executive Council is the only policymaking body. It is made up of the state governor, the military commander in the state capital, representatives from the navy and air force, and the state commissioner of police. The commissioners at the state level (the equivalent of ministers at the federal level) are also members. The council meetings are chaired by the governor.

At the local level, the Local Government Council is the highest policymaking body. It makes decision on all matters affecting entire communities in the local government area. Though the existence of local government is recognized in the constitution, its autonomy is limited by frequent interventions from the state government. The interventions are usually in the areas of budgetary control, jurisdictional control, and personnel matters.

The ephemeral nature of the policymaking machinery in the Nigerian political system has contributed greatly to public policy failure. Each succeeding government has tended to modify inherited structures and processes or create new ones in order to address a new reality. The 1988 civil service reforms, for instance, were designed in large measure to facilitate the implementation of the government's structural adjustment program.

The 1988 Civil Service Reforms

Given the problems and failures of the policymaking process, the 1988 civil service reforms were designed to enhance policy management, generate higher productivity, and ease implementation problems of the government's structural adjustment policies. The reforms rest on four pillars: politicizing the upper echelons of the civil service; professionalizing the remainder of the civil service; improving the performance, productivity, and responsiveness of civil servants; and enhancing public accountability. In particular, the reform provisions relating to professionalization require every officer to specialize. A major advantage of the latter is that officers have a more profound understanding of the responsibilities of their ministries, thereby enhancing their efficiency and productivity.

Introduced in January 1988, the reforms have not taken root in all the states of the federation, making it difficult to generalize. Although some states and the federal government have made bold efforts to implement the reform measures effectively, other states have hesitated to initiate reforms. Explanations for their slow progress have included lack of funds and shortages of personnel and equipment. Due to the unevenness of the reforms, not much has really changed in the policymaking process.

Where reforms have occurred, central ministers and their counterparts at the state level now exert greater influence over policy formulation and implementation. Nevertheless, the civil service still shares in the initiation, formulation, and execution of public policies. The person who appears to have lost out under the new dispensation is the director general of a ministry, whose status has now been reduced from that of chief executive and accounting officer to that of second in command in a ministry or department.

Another result of the reform efforts has been increased reliance on ad hoc bodies in policymaking. In particular, committees have risen to prominence with mandates that focus on new issues as well as the resolution of old problems. A greater proportion of the functionaries in these committees is drawn from outside the civil service, but the bureaucracy continues to provide technical support and assistance to the committees. Thus, the civil service remains critical to the policymaking process.

In general, public policymaking in present-day Nigeria conforms to a familiar pattern found in other African countries, although there have been some visible deviations. In spite of the reforms over the past twenty years, the Nigerian civil service continues to be characterized by what Joseph calls "cronyism" and "prebendalism" in which patron-client relationships and personalistic loyalties influence the policymaking process.[4] The following section examines more fully the process of policymaking in Nigeria.

The Process of Policymaking

In idealized form Nigeria has developed a process of policymaking that is conducive to development management at both the macro- and the microlevels. Much remains to be done, however, to put into operation the processes of decisionmaking and implementation. The policy cycle as it is presently constituted has both strengths and weaknesses:

Problem identification. At this initial stage in the policy process certain conditions in society are perceived and defined as problems and are accepted as policy issues that government is eventually forced to do something about. The task of converting a societal problem into a public issue and calling government attention to it is a crucial aspect of the Nigerian national political process.

The task of articulating and aggregating the interests of the people is accomplished through organized pressure groups such as the Manufacturers' Association of Nigeria (MAN) and through public opinion and the mass media. The civil service has also played a leading role in this respect, and more recently, ad hoc committees are becoming sources of aggregated interest claims.

Policy formulation. Once an issue has been accepted on the government's policy agenda a number of activities are likely to occur, although the formulation of public policy proposals remains an activity carried out by the executive arm of government (see above). Depending on its scale, complexity, and urgency, the policy issue is submitted for careful study and research within the bureaucracy or by an ad hoc committee of experts. Recommendations are then presented to the executive for consideration.

At this stage all the key technical and some nontechnical dimensions of the issue are closely scrutinized and assessed, and data are generated that help to shed light on possible causes and solutions. Proposed policies are then identified, and their technical soundness and desirability analyzed and ascertained. The goals of the policy are prioritized, the means of achieving them identified, the time requirements for each goal established, and the physical and human resource requirements determined.

Many of the above activities take place in the ministries. In ministries where a mandatory Department of Planning, Research, and Statistics has been established, the department plays a crucial role in policy formulation. A cabinet committee, comprising the minister, director general, and other directors, oversees the activities of the department in policy matters. In ministries where the relationship of the chief executive and the director general is not cordial, the cabinet is a one-man committee, with the minister issuing orders directly to department heads with or without the knowledge of his deputy.

Legitimation. Legislative action is necessary (almost indispensable) in the Nigerian policymaking process. It accords the proposed policy political support, legality, and legitimacy. Whether or not the policy proposal gets adopted depends a great deal on the value preferences of the dominant groups or coalition in the legislative body. Legislative authorization also ensures that an appropriation or requisite resource allocation is made for the successful implementation of the policy.

Policy implementation. Once a policy is formulated and legitimated it must be implemented in a sustained and effective manner in order to create the desired impact. Sustainability and effectiveness are contingent on the caliber of the human resources available, the quality and relevance of the policy design and proposal, and popular political support for the policy action. Indeed, the political dimension in Nigeria has been critical in the attainment of sustainability and effectiveness and is characterized by the undue influence of specialized interests. It is this political dimension that tends to be ignored and underrated in management development strategies, and, combined with weaknesses within the civil service, it limits the effectiveness of the Nigerian process of policymaking as described above.

Policy evaluation. The advantage of policy evaluation is that it is a learning process. Evaluation enables policymakers to record their experiences for future use, and information gathered from the exercise forms the basis for adjusting existing policy. In an incrementalist policy process the new information forms part of the data base available for future policy considerations.

In Nigeria there is no serious effort to evaluate policies. This is one of the factors contributing to frequent policy failures. Even in cases where government has evaluated public policies, the exercise did not have an impact on the policy. This has been the experience of the National Institute for Policy and Strategic Studies (NIPSS). Likewise, policy evaluation efforts in the ministries has been sporadic and inefficient. The civil service reforms envisage that the Department of Planning, Research, and Statistics will be involved in policy evaluation, but the department is still in its embryonic stage.

A review of the policymaking framework in Nigeria reveals that the policymaking process has not yet evolved regularized procedures or the institutional structures for mobilizing popular involvement or for generating widespread consultation in policy development.

Two programs of the present government stand out as exceptions to the above tendency: the structural adjustment program and the transition to civil rule program. In both cases there was widespread consultation with the people as they were called upon to debate and submit recommendations to government on policy preference. These debates generated considerable interest and participation of the people, and the policy decisions of government were heavily influenced by this popular consultation.

A policy decision in which there was minimal consultation with stakeholders was the decision to establish the National Directorate of Employment. The directorate was created to mitigate the pains of the structural adjustment program through the generation of employment opportunities. In 1985 the government directed the ministries in charge of employment, labor, and productivity; education; social development, youth, and sports; and national planning to collaborate with state governments and the organized private sector to produce strategies for dealing with mass unemployment, with special attention given to school leavers.

A committee of twenty-seven members was constituted; but almost all of the members, including the chairman, were civil servants. The committee was guided in its deliberations by the working papers and proposals submitted by the various ministries, state governments, and the organized private sector. There was no visible contact with the stakeholders during the early stages of policy development. It was primarily a civil service activity.

Capacity Building Through Training and the Civil Service Reforms

This section examines capacity building in Nigeria through human resource development, with particular reference to the 1988 civil service reforms.

The dominant role of government in a modern welfare-oriented state such as Nigeria has called into question the capacity of the civil service to manage the system effectively and efficiently. It should be noted, however, that because policy management involves both policy formulation and policy implementation, capacity problems are not restricted to the civil service. Policy management also requires well-informed and capable political leaders. The problems of policymaking in Nigeria are the result of many factors and, in particular, include the following.

The policymaking process is structurally diffuse. Although this diffusion may not necessarily pose much difficulty at the policy formulation stage, it is likely to do so at the policy implementation stage. For example, there are many bodies implementing government policies in health, education, security, and other sectors. This problem is compounded by the fact that policy-planning expertise is scarce in the country, both inside and outside of government. Among the organized interest groups who are expected to influence the determination of policy issues and the formulation of policy, little capacity exists for policy analysis. A similar situation is evident in the various government agencies expected to make technical contributions to the policy formulation process and who have responsibility for policy execution and evaluation.

Policy knowledge is inadequate. A major problem area in the policymaking process is the lack of quality data, without which policymaking is forced to rely unduly on guesswork or even on the personal or idiosyncratic preferences of the policymakers. Planning without facts has become the bane of policymaking in Nigeria. The uncoordinated nature of the work of the various data gathering and research institutions in the country has been further complicated by political corruption, all of which has seriously distorted information gathering and policy analysis activities.

Power is imbalanced. Another major problem reflects the lack of balance in power among political executives and their top bureaucrats. For many years the bureaucrats have exerted a disproportionate influence on policymaking. The crucial issue concerning the role of public administrators in policymaking in Nigeria is not whether they will continue to be actively and centrally involved in initiating, formulating, and implementing policies. Rather, the issue has focused on how public administrators can be transformed from an essentially powerful and anonymous class-based group, oriented primarily toward compliance with regulations and adherence to procedures, into a committed, effective force for social change and sustained, mass-based economic development.

The historical record offers no indication that further education and retraining or approaches that rely on bureaucratic initiative and voluntary compliance will provide the basis for a reorientation of the public services in this direction. Deeper politicization and tighter control of the bureaucracy by democratically elected civilian leaders appear to be more promising avenues for effecting such a transformation. The current civil service reforms appear to have entrenched political supremacy over the bureaucracy, assuming the ascendancy of a democratically elected civilian government. It is claimed that the recent economic crises in the country have been traceable, at least in part, to the power imbalance between the political and professional executives.

Public-private sector relationships lack openness and transparency. Project implementation failures often can be traced to the relationship between the principal actors in the public and private sectors. Multinational corporations and companies, consultancy firms, and construction companies operating in the country constitute a formidable force in the process of government program execution.[5] Various investigations carried out at different times in the past have clearly demonstrated that government officials and private sector organizations have often acted in collusion to defraud government of a substantial part of the financial resources allocated for the execution of public projects. Corruption remains a major policy issue in Nigeria and is present at many different stages and levels of the policy process.

Civil service capacity needs to be strengthened. Given these problems in the policymaking process, it is necessary to enhance policy management skills. Increased attention to capacity building and the civil service reforms in general are also necessary to guarantee the success of the economic recovery program and other structural adjustment policies. At issue is the country's need to strengthen institutional capacity for policy analysis, formulation, and implementation, and the need to imbue every civil servant with a sense of purpose and urgency.[6]

The need for a professionalized civil service and the performance focus of the civil service reforms has placed staff training in much bolder relief than before. In order to improve efficiency in the operation of the ministries and to raise the performance standards of employees, each ministry has been required to operate and maintain employee training programs within or under a particular ministry.[7]

The 1988 civil service reforms were a comprehensive package of provisions that aimed at enhancing the capacity of the Nigerian bureaucracy. After the reforms had been promulgated, the Office of Management Services and Training (OMS&T) recognized that it would be difficult to meet these aspirations unless the nation first adopted a training policy to guide all human resource development. It was against this background that the OMS&T organized a national conference on human resource development and utilization in March 1989. The conference was a critical first step in a series of activities that would lead to the emergence of a virile and dynamic human resource development and utilization policy for Nigeria.

The emphasis that the new reforms have placed on the professionalization of the civil service was a conscious attempt to enhance the capacities of public officials in policy management. Capacity building is also reflected in the new dispensation that requires officers to make their careers entirely in the ministry or department of their choice. This directive will enable them to acquire the necessary expertise and experience through relevant specialized training and uninterrupted involvement with the work of their respective ministry or department. Research has shown that this provision is a welcome attempt at capacity building.[8]

With regard to promotions, performance has been emphasized over seniority. A total promotion rating scale of 100 percent now allots 95 percent to performance (based on interviews and additional qualifications and examinations) and only 5 percent to seniority. Such changes, if implemented, provide evidence of the extent to which government is determined to build the capacity of public officials in policy management.

The reforms have also emphasized the regular flow of staff between the public service and the private sector. This development is based on the belief that ideas and experiences shared between the two sectors can assist in enhancing productivity in the public service.

The main strategy by which the government is attempting to build capacity in policy analysis emphasizes civil service training.[9] The number of public officers, including ministers and directors general, attending training programs has increased tremendously since 1988, when the reforms were launched. The number of workshops, conferences, and seminars organized since 1988 has also increased. Although overseas training programs continue to be sponsored, more attention is being focused on training public officers at local institutions. The two most favored institutions are NIPSS, based in Jos, and the Administrative Staff College of Nigeria (ASCON), based in Lagos. The former focuses on policy issues, and ASCON emphasizes the development of policy implementation strategies and skills.

Conclusion

The policy process of initiation, formulation, implementation, and evaluation constitutes a four-step cycle. The successful completion of the policy cycle is contingent upon both an institutional capacity and human resource capability. In the case of Nigeria, institutional capacity outside of government is nonexistent. Much of public policy–related activity remains within the exclusive preserve of the civil service.

A new trend is emerging, however, in which the organized private sector and ad hoc bodies composed of members outside the civil service now contribute to the policy process. For example, the political transition program originated from the recommendations of one such body, the Political Bureau (a mixed government/nongovernment committee), and has been highly successful.

The future role of the civil service will be critical to increasing the capacity of the Nigerian state to promote economic and social development. It is not a question of whether the civil service will be involved in the initiation and formulation of development policy. Rather, the question is how the civil service can be transformed from a powerful, special-interest and class-based group that operates on the basis of patronage and corruption to a transparent and effective agent that can promote policy changes and economic and social development.

There is both promise and potential danger in attempts to

reform the civil service in Nigeria. On the one hand, the reforms are designed to increase the capacity of the bureaucracy to promote economic and social change. On the other hand, the civil service has a history of personalistic decisionmaking and self-promotion as it makes and implements policy. These contradictory tendencies need to be reconciled as the country moves toward civilian government and political transparency.[10] Given the continued debt and economic difficulties facing Nigeria in the 1990s and beyond, the country's policymaking process will continue to be of concern to international development agencies such as the IMF and the World Bank.

Notes

1. A number of core activities have been recognized and accepted as the responsibilities of the state. These are security, regulation, the provision of services, and socioeconomic development. How the state is organized to achieve specified objectives determines the management of public policy. Public policy can be viewed as a set of processes through which policies are initiated, formulated, implemented, sustained, and evaluated. Through such processes, the state is able to perform and achieve results. See Merilee S. Grindle, ed., *Politics and Policy Implementation in the Third World* (Princeton, N.J.: Princeton University Press, 1980), for a discussion of public policy processes.

2. On recent events in Nigeria see Richard A. Joseph, *Democracy and Prebendal Politics in Nigeria: The Rise and Fall of the Second Republic* (New York: Cambridge University Press, 1987); Larry Diamond, *Class, Ethnicity and Democracy in Nigeria* (Syracuse, N.Y.: Syracuse University Press, 1988); Thomas J. Biersteker, *Multinationals, the State, and Control of the Nigerian Economy* (Princeton, N.J.: Princeton University Press, 1987); and Sayre Schatz, *Nigerian Capitalism* (Berkeley: University of California Press, 1977). Thomas Callaghy compared Nigerian structural adjustment efforts with those in Ghana and Zambia. See his "Lost Between State and Market: The Politics of Economic Adjustment in Ghana, Zambia, and Nigeria," in *Economic Crisis and Policy Choice: The Politics of Adjustment in the Third World*, ed. Joan M. Nelson (Princeton, N.J.: Princeton University Press, 1990), pp. 257–319.

3. In particular, Edgar Pisani had concerns about externally imposed free-market conditions in the African context: "If the state did not support the national reality which is in the process of emerging, if there was no national protectionism opposed to completely deregulated international markets, the economy of the developing countries would be in a worse state than it is today. To simply and clearly preach obedience to the law of the market place is to wish to impede the establishment of an African agriculture and economy; to speak of enterprises is too often to speak of foreign enterprises and to encourage their conquering advances." Edgar Pisani, "Accessibility and Sensitivity of Public Administration" (paper presented at the International Conference of the International Institute of Administrative Sciences, Marrakesh, Morocco, August 1990), p. 27.

4. Joseph, *Democracy and Prebendal Politics.*

5. See Thomas Biersteker's analysis of the role of multinational corporations, local business, and state actors in *Multinationals, the State, and Control of the Nigerian Economy.*

6. Callaghy, "Lost Between State and Market," p. 261.

7. See Section 4(1) and 4(2) of Decree 43 (Abuja: Government of Nigeria, 1988).

8. Jerald Hage and Kurt Finsterbusch, *Organizational Change as a Development Strategy: Models and Tactics for Improving Third World Organizations* (Boulder, Colo.: Lynne Rienner Publishers, 1987), pp. 77–78 and 241–242. On the other hand, Guy Peters warned against a professional value system that places professional loyalties above that of the administrative and political systems as a whole. See B. Guy Peters, *The Politics of Bureaucracy*, 3rd ed. (New York: Longman, 1989), pp. 276–277.

9. Training, as defined by the United Nations Educational, Scientific, and Cultural Organisation (UNESCO) Report on Mass Communication, No. 73 (Paris: UNESCO, 1975), involves a planning process to influence attitudes and transmit the skills necessary to induce the effective communication of ideas, information sharing, and experience transfer.

10. The abrogation of Nigeria's June 12, 1993, elections by the military regime brings this change into question.

4

Zambia: Form Versus Substance in the One-Party State

Gatian F. Lungu & Mulenga C. Bwalya

Writing about politics and policymaking in Zambia today is a daunting though interesting and exciting exercise.[1] First, like much of the rest of Africa, there has been a general absence of a policy analysis perspective or tradition in Zambia. Second, Zambia has entered the era of political pluralism, which engenders its own problems of analysis. Finally, public policies have generally been approached from a development planning perspective and within the context of macroeconomics. Rarely has the interdisciplinary nature and the institutional arrangements and rearrangements necessary for effective policy analysis, implementation, and evaluation been given adequate attention. It would not be surprising, for example, if one failed to find literature on Zambian public policy that specifically refers to or prescribes institutional operational capacities for policy implementation, change, and sustainability. This gap renders it difficult to confidently present the Zambian case.

With the introduction of pluralism in October 1991,[2] many writers have been carried away with speculation about what things will or should be like after the change of government. Such speculation has neither concrete evidence nor a sustainable foundation. It was this profound dilemma that persuaded us to examine what has been in existence over the past seventeen years, namely, public policy in one-party Zambia, reflecting on the experiences of capacity building for policy change and sustainability. The policy successes and failures of the one-party state should provide an interesting analytical framework, especially with the return to a multiparty state and with all the hopes, expectations, and dangers that accompany such a mammoth transition.

Public Policymaking in Zambia

The Institutional Arrangements

Zambia has applied a mixed approach to the policy process. The adoption of a combination of approaches has been both the cause and the result of the nature of the institutions themselves and the institutional arrangements made for policymaking. Consequently, in theory the government comprises a complex array of institutions organized in various and appropriate ways to ensure that relevant, realistic, and balanced policies are formulated in which goals are matched with resources and strategies are put forth for goal achievement. The reality, however, has not lived up to the aspirations of those who designed Zambia's policymaking bodies.

Political Institutions

In the one-party system that existed in Zambia from 1973 to 1991, the organ at the apex of the system was the United National Independence Party (UNIP). According to Article 7 of the UNIP Constitution: "The party is the supreme organization and the guiding political force in the land. Its main task and objectives as expressed in Article 4 shall provide guidelines for all persons and institutions in the Republic."[3]

It is instructive here to note the key words: "shall provide guidelines for *all persons and institutions in the Republic.*" These words denote that the party (UNIP) was both the source and confluence of policies in the nation and therefore was supreme. Further, as Article 8 of the constitution enunciates, "no law, regulation or Act shall be enacted, passed or done by any state organ which is in conflict or inconsistent with the National Policies of the Party."[4] Thus, all Zambian policymaking institutions, whether party, government, or nongovernmental, were to draw guidelines from and operate within the broad policy provisions of the party. We must hasten to point out here that although the party was supreme in accordance with the philosophy of humanism, it was not above human beings. Rather, it was supposed to be a tool or an instrument for the service of humans.[5]

The party operated through a hierarchical series of ordinarily elective national and local organs. At the apex of the five national organs was the Party Congress, followed by the National Council, the Central Committee, the Committee of Chairmen, and the Party Control Commission. The local organs were more numerous (thirteen in all) and ranged from provincial committees down to section councils.

The Party Congress, known as the General Conference until 1988, met once every five years and was the supreme policymaking organ of the party and government. Its wide membership included all members of the National Council and up to 600 delegates from each province. Its main functions included: the election of the president and members of the Central Committee of the party; the definition and orientation of general policies for the nation's development; and the formulation, revision, and the consideration and approval of national development plans. Operating as the organ for formulating general policy and guidelines of both the party and the government, the decisions of the Party Congress were considered "valid and obligatory to the Party, Government and public institutions and [could] only be revoked or altered by the Party Congress."[6]

During the interval between one Party Congress and the next, the National Council of the party assumed the mantle of policymaking at its yearly meetings. Through several committees covering important national policy areas, the council had the responsibility to:

1. Direct the activities of all organs of the party and the state within the framework of the principles and resolutions passed by the Party Congress;
2. Determine the political line for the implementation of party policies, review and appraise party programs and national development plans, reappraise the legal and sociocultural organization and development of the country; and
3. Approve candidates for the office of president of the party and members of the Central Committee.

The inclusion in the National Council of groups such as permanent secretaries; district executive secretaries; senior officers from the state house, the party headquarters, and the cabinet office; chiefs of the defense and security forces; and so on, was an effort to integrate at the highest level of policy formulation the technocratic, defense, and security organs of government. The goal was to inject the necessary technocratic inputs into the policy analysis process.

Next there was the Central Committee of the party, with its inner circle Committee of Chairmen of subcommittees of the Central Committee, whose job was to further concretize the broad policies and guidelines emanating from the National Council. Beginning in 1988 the composition of the Central Committee was increased to sixty-eight members, consisting of forty-one members elected by the Party Congress, seven members appointed by the president of the party, and not more than twenty cabinet ministers. The inclusion of twenty cabinet ministers and seven appointed members in the Central Committee was intended to ensure that technocrats and professionals with expertise in relevant policy areas were included. This allocation also allowed for the participation of both technocrats and politicians at the highest levels of policy formulation.

Indeed, through the twenty-three-member Committee of Chairmen (under the chairmanship of the president of the party), the Central Committee ensured not only that major policy areas were identified and specific policies analyzed but also that decisions regarding the running of the party and government were made and concretized. Again, it is important to note that each of the ten subcommittees (of the Committee of Chairmen) was not only responsible for a particular policy area (for example, defense and security, social and cultural, rural development, and so on), but it also was supported by up to six technocrat/professional advisers competent in a relevant subject area. In addition, after 1989, the secretaries of the subcommittees were experienced and competent technocrats or professionals at the permanent secretary level.

At the 1988 national conference another organ, the Party Control Commission, was added to the list. It consisted of eleven members, and its main function was to monitor party, government, and state-owned enterprises and see that they understood and actively implemented party policies, decisions, plans, directives, and programs. The commission became the watchdog of the party and government, overseeing that all arms of the government operated within the policy guidelines of the party.

Below the national organs there were thirteen local party organs whose main functions included: organizing the party; explaining and publicizing party policies and programs; planning, guiding, and supervising all development and financial activities; instilling a spirit of hard work and self-reliance; and mobilizing the people for socioeconomic and political development in their areas of jurisdiction. These levels also followed the principle of integrating technocrats and politicians. Ideally, the decisions arising from the local organs should have been based on objective and rational analysis.

Government Institutions

Although the main function of the government was to implement the policies of the party, it was not entirely excluded from the policymaking function. As we have noted above, government officers (technocrats) participated in the policymaking process through their membership in the various party organs. Through these various organs the government did, in fact, play a policy formulation and articulation role in its own right, in addition to its traditional policy implementation function.

The organs through which government performed its functions included: the National Assembly, the cabinet ministries and departments, provincial and district administrations, parastatal bodies, and other agencies of the government in different sectors of the national economy. These organs, like those of the party, were organized hierarchically from national level down to the grassroots in the form of ministries, departments, provinces, districts, sections, stations, and camps. Although policy analysis transcends the entire spectrum of the government structure, the main organs of policy analysis were supposed to be the National Assembly, the cabinet and cabinet office, the National Commission for Development Planning, and the Ministry of Finance and other central ministries.

The extent to which the National Assembly was a party or government organ tended to be complicated by the nature of the assembly's composition in a one-party state. In fact, it was aligned to the government hierarchy by virtue of Parliament being one of the three arms of government (the executive, the judicial, and the legislative). The National Assembly, therefore, was not, strictly speaking, a policy-formulating organ; rather, it was a policy-legitimatizing, -legalizing, and -enabling organ. Like the courts and service commissions, the National Assembly was more or less an independent organ of the party and the government, which ensured the translation of policy resolutions and guidelines for implementation into binding legal instruments and directions for governmental actions. Without the legislative seal, party policies could not be translated into practical policy outcomes by the government machinery. Thus, the assembly empowered the government's policy-implementing organs to implement party policies. It had a significant influence on policymaking because legally the National Assembly could refuse to sanction or implement funding for policies that it did not support.

Although the cabinet and the ministerial structures that flowed from it were primarily party policy-implementing organs, they were also policy-influencing bodies. Through membership in the cabinet and various cabinet committees, ministers, and other officials or technocrats were given the privilege of helping formulate party and government policy on all subjects, since it was through the cabinet and cabinet committees that broad party policies and programs were put into operation. At the same time, these were also the bodies through which suggestions from the ministries, departments, and government agencies were discussed and crystallized for parliamentary consideration. These discussions included the nonworkability of policies, or alternative ways for the implementation of policies.

The National Commission for Development Planning (NCDP)[7] acted as a central planning agency translating party policy into concrete and comprehensive national development plans. The commission also took into consideration contributions from other government organs and the private sector and consulted with the budget office. The NCDP also coordinated the policy analysis process and arranged that planning data and resources were made available by the relevant ministries or through other sources. It was also responsible for monitoring the progress of all development programs in the country as well as being the body through which requests for foreign development assistance could be channeled.

The ministries, provinces, and parastatal organizations formed the technocratic bodies for the practical implementation of policies. As technocratic organizations they followed a bureaucratic model.[8] The parastatal organizations also emphasized profit making. In practice, of course, the bureaucratic model was mediated and hindered from performing as well as it could by various environmental factors (for example, political interference, corruption, and nepotism) as well as the failure of the system to provide properly qualified, competent, highly committed, and ethically grounded personnel.

The party and government organs were connected and formally interacted in many ways. First, the prime minister and his ministers were also members of the Central Committee of the party. Second, the Central Committee and cabinet held so-called joint meetings once every month. Third, the Committee of Chairmen had representatives from both organs. In general, there were various opportunities for close interaction between party and government in policy formulation through their supervision of the large policy areas covered by the ministries and the parastatal sector.

The Process

From a national perspective, policymaking in Zambia has taken a two-pronged approach. The official position under UNIP was that policymaking would be conducted through a decentralized and participatory process. However, a fusion of a centralized policy approach and a decentralized policy approach existed (that is, up-down and down-up), which was supported and consolidated by rational, technocratic analyses. In principle this meant that both general and specific policy issues, problems, and suggestions were discussed and progressively screened for relevance, soundness, consistency, political correctness, and so on, by both political and technocratic groups through a variety of institutions before being crystallized and prioritized into policy options.[9] Depending upon the magnitude, sensitivity, or hierarchical/geographical coverage of each policy adopted, it was pronounced by and allocated to any of several party and government levels for action.

In general, there was a system of mutually complementary and interactive policymaking between the political and bureaucratic-technocratic hierarchies. The political hierarchy was concerned with the social, subjective, integrative conflict resolution and survival interests of public policies. The concern was to ensure that the social values and expectations of the predominant ideology or philosophy in the society were fulfilled. On the other hand, the bureaucratic-technocratic hierarchy was more concerned with the specific, goal-oriented options of society that were economic, rational, input minimizing, and output maximizing.[10] Through the interactive and consultative policymaking processes among the two hierarchies, balanced policies (taking into account relevant social, political, and economic realities) should have emerged. In this way practically all the basic policy documents, such as the party manifestos or guidelines, national development plans, annual budgets, and so forth, should have been discussed and the necessary inputs obtained at the various levels of the two hierarchies before adoption.

In terms of local or sectoral policies, the approach was to deal with them at the local and sectoral levels so long as they did not significantly differ from or conflict with broad national policy guidelines. The establishment of the integrated local administration system (headed by a political appointee) in 1980 was done precisely to support and ensure that policymaking (at least for issues of local or sectoral significance) was done through a decentralized approach. Similar to what occurred at the national level, an integrated approach between the political and technocratic hierarchies was provided for at the local and sectoral levels, with policy issues subjected to both political and technocratic scrutiny before adoption.

In practice, however, some of these provisions were not always followed. For example, "ad hoc–ism" occurred to a considerable extent throughout the period of Kaunda's presidency, with the president making sudden decisions in emotional outbursts at public meetings and without the benefit of counsel.

There have been many cases where what we have termed the "political/integrative/subjective" approach has led to policies being announced in public before being subjected to the "economic/rational/analytical" process. Without proper scrutiny and detailed knowledge of the range of policy options and probable implications, policy issues have emerged as national policies in political addresses and declarations delivered at various occasions. Often this was done to satisfy the social-psychological needs and expectations of the audience or for political or ideological expediency.

Two recent and related examples of "ad hoc–ism" seem appropriate to examine. At a press conference held at the State House on November 2, 1988, President Kaunda announced: (1) the setting up of a housing conglomerate to take charge of government housing, and (2) the transfer of the erstwhile Civil Service Mechanical Services Department (MSD) to ZIMCO (Zambia Industrial and Mining Corporation) and directed that it be split into provincial companies. The president then went on to note that "what I want to see is that civil servants get good housing allowances and find themselves housing." Current government houses "must be for rent, doing business parastatal wise. We must succeed, we cannot fail."[11] Regarding MSD, the president announced that the government would hold 51 percent of the shares; private capital would take the rest. It was also announced that foreign investors would provide machinery and general managers for the next five years.

The intention and rationale of these policy pronouncements were well meaning. The president wanted not only good and efficient housing and mechanical services for the public service and the populace at large, but he also wanted the new organizations to operate on profit lines, generating their own incomes and standing on their own feet. This action was meant to end government subsidies to these organizations, freeing more investment for other public ventures or for deficit reduction. In the end, the government would be able to provide an adequate, viable, and efficient service to the people. Strangely enough, however, the newly appointed top managers were instead directed not only to study and propose workable structures and ways and means of making the organizations operate; they were further required to scout around for suitable investors and initial funds to enable them to start operating.

This is an example of both the social/subjective and ad hoc approaches to policymaking. The policy pronouncements seemed to be little more than politically expedient, thinly veiled responses to and pacification of the growing mass of vocal people who had been persistent in their complaints about the shortages and inadequacy of housing or the mediocre services rendered by MSD.

The nature of the pronouncements clearly negated any possibility of the a priori subjection of overtly desired social and economic needs to rational scrutiny in order to arrive at policy options; their social, economic, and political implications; the types and sources of resources; and the institutional arrangements needed to implement the options.

Not surprisingly, both policy directives have met with difficulties in implementation. Moreover, the policy pronouncements were made without outlining the corresponding organizational structures; without definite knowledge of and concrete arrangements for the types of resources required, their availability, and their source; and without stipulating the institutional arrangements, operational rules, and the standards of measurement of their goal attainment levels. In the case of housing, apart from the director general's post there was no provision for support staff, which hindered the immediate implementation of the policy. At the same time the new organization was dependent on economic rents; yet no corresponding arrangements were (or have been) made to adjust the housing allowances of civil servants to levels that would enable them to pay the economic rents expected, most likely because the government probably had no extra funds. Lack of clear guidelines and the inadequacy or lack of skilled personnel only aggravated the situation, needlessly delaying policy implementation.

There is another hindrance to the practical application of a balanced approach to policymaking. The measures taken to institute a more decentralized approach to policymaking somewhat constrained the process. Because of the relatively low degree of integration between the center and the periphery, national leaders remained suspicious of decentralized power and the extent to which local leaders wanted to exercise direct control. On the other hand, local leaders saw this as interference in and attempts at usurpation of power by the national leadership. Mistrust reigned between the center and the periphery, limiting commitment to policy implementation. The competition for power between national and local leaders meant wasted efforts spent in fending off real or imagined threats to authority at the expense of policy implementation.

Given the significant resource constraints in Zambia, compounded by the high costs of mobilization and coordination of highly decentralized systems as well as the sometimes overt apathy observable among local potential participants, some national leaders and technocrats have tended to see the decentralized approach as too wasteful and inefficient to merit their support. Among these doubting Thomases there has been an absence of committed and concerted effort to see the policies succeed.

Capacity Building for Policy Change and Sustainability

The Status Quo

The discussion of policymaking institutions has shown that arrangements during the Kaunda period emerged from a series of reform measures to improve the capacity of political and technocratic institutions in formulating and implementing policies. The reforms have been predicated largely on the greater integration of political and technocratic elements to improve objectivity, effectiveness, and efficiency in the formulation and implementation of policies. For example, we have seen the deliberate widening of the membership of the Central Committee of the party from the original twenty-five members to sixty-eight members to include a sizable number of seasoned technocrats holding very high, influential, and strategic positions in the government; parastatals (including mining companies); and the private business and trade union sectors.

Second, the party leadership created a committee[12] to co-ordinate and supervise the formulation and implementation of national party policies. They also established the Party Control Commission to monitor the administration of policies as well as to periodically recommend areas of improvement in the policy development and implementation process.

Third, we noted the reorganization of ministries to reduce their size, activities, and staff contingents to improve coordination and reduce operational costs. The Ministry of Finance, for example, was merged with and swallowed the NCDP, and the Division of Science and Technology has been added to the Ministry of Higher Education. There have also been actions such as the hiving off of ministries, departments, or divisions and establishing them as independent corporations or companies operating on free-market principles. As examples of the latter, we noted the experiences of the Mechanical Services Department and the Public Housing Division of the Public Works Department.

Fourth, key planning and policy monitoring institutions were strengthened. Examples include the Ministry of Finance's efforts to strengthen the NCDP and to upgrade the budget office; the transfer of the division for decentralization to the cabinet office; and the creation of provincial and district planning units throughout the country to coordinate and advise on development planning activities at the lower levels of the policy process.

The structural arrangements and organic composition of the new institutions were not only relevant and conducive to rational, effective, and efficient public policy formulation and implementation, but they were also in keeping with the socialist-oriented national philosophy of humanism defined by President Kaunda and UNIP. Admittedly, most of these measures were put in place before the 1991 elections, making it difficult for a fair evaluation of their impact on the policy process. Even so, it is possible on the basis of previous experience to make an ex-ante evaluation of the impact and sustainability of such changes, if only to have a clear prognosis of likely things to come.

The Constraints

In the past one of the major factors affecting the quality of policymaking and successful policy implementation and sustainability *has not been the structural aspect,* but, rather, the process aspect. By process, we refer to a whole matrix of intraorganizational factors including choice and organization of activities, planning, time management, consultation, discipline, grievance handling, delegation, learning, and, above all, decisionmaking. The lack of appropriate skills in these areas has meant that even simple problems or nonproblems can halt the process of genuine, well-informed policymaking or effective implementation from taking place. Both the formulation and implementation of policy require highly skilled, competent, perceptive, flexible, strong, and effective management personnel at all levels of the policy implementation process.

Human resources. The common experience regarding management personnel within the civil service is that they are often weak, misplaced, frightened, frustrated, and often uncommitted to the policies of the nation. Such behavior is not conducive to effective and rational policy formulation, implementation, and sustainability, even when the appropriate institutional structures exist. As Ollawa has observed, the typical behavior of such personnel under these circumstances is to base their judgments on an assessment of their superiors' (politicians) interest in the matter, or whether their superiors have taken a public stance on the matter.[13]

The management attitudes observed by Ollawa can be the result of several factors: gross misplacement of personnel in an effort to effect ethnic balancing; the lack of properly qualified and skilled staff; and the very poor salaries and conditions of service found in the public sector. Regarding the latter, a typical civil servant with similar qualifications and experience often will receive a salary three times smaller than his/her parastatal counterpart, and up to six times less than his/her private sector counterpart, and without any fringe benefits. In view of the worsening economic situation in Zambia, with galloping inflation and the resultant high cost of living, the civil service offers little incentive to engender commitment and productivity on a sustainable basis.

To be sure, the Zambian government has employed many qualified personnel in ministries and parastatal companies. The problem is that these are too few and they are often deployed in jobs they were not trained for, making it extremely difficult for them to have a meaningful impact. Moreover, qualified personnel do not stay long in government employment due to the poor conditions of service. Consequently, overall human resources are underqualified, with the result that government capacity to formulate and implement policies is seriously impaired. In local government, for example, many district councils do not have qualified engineers, accountants, or economists, let alone planners, so that even ordinary routine duties are not adequately attended to.

Finance and infrastructure. Even if Zambia had well-placed, skilled, and competent personnel manning the policymaking and policy-implementing organs of the party and the government, their impact would not be great because they would lack the basic tools and instruments of their trade. Again, the discouraging economic environment observed earlier precludes the procurement of an appropriate and adequate policy infrastructure (for example, computers, transport, and communication facilities).

Many policies also have floundered due to the inadequate financial resources that are required to implement them. For instance, the educational reforms proposed in 1976–1977 stalled in the 1980s, partly due to inadequate funding for extending the years of compulsory basic education from seven to nine years. One of the problems leading to inadequate financing is that many policies are designed without financial consideration. The educational reform proposals furnish an excellent example of a public policy that was vigorously formulated but lacked a budget.

Undercosting of policies is another problem. The case of food coupons, announced in 1990, is one such example. The cost of food coupons was calculated during the policy formulation stage, but the costs for administering the program were ignored. The basic and underlying problem in Zambia, however, is the poverty that exists to a confounding degree. Since the collapse of the copper-based economy in the mid-1970s, the financing of almost all development policies has been extremely difficult.

Donors have come to the rescue on several occasions, but this has increased the external debt and resulted in the devaluation of the national currency. The involvement of international lenders and donors in financing development policies has also created pressure for the Zambian government to resort to strategies that exclude popular participation. Adjustment programs, for example, are merely announced to the nation, and the government appears to have little say in the formulation of these economic adjustment policies.

Reorganization fever. An additional constraint in Zambia has been the incessant tendency for reorganization. Although policy change is a necessary and important element in creating a responsive policymaking system, too much change can be detrimental and counterproductive. Too frequent reorganizations, reshuffling, and transfers of structures, functions, and personnel not only create turbulence in the policy system, they also hinder continuity and breed insecurity and uncertainty. Unless structures are given time to institutionalize, they will be of little importance to the capacity building process.

Some of the reform measures have already had counterproductive effects. For instance, the reduction of the retirement age of civil servants and reductions in the civil service personnel establishment have not had, at least in the short run, the intended effect of improving the efficiency of the civil service. On the contrary, retirements and pruning exercises have left ministries, departments, and agencies with not only young and largely inexperienced personnel but also with fewer numbers. All of this is occurring at a time when the tasks of government are increasing in both size and complexity. Over the past few years these actions have contributed to both poorly analyzed policies and a slowdown in the pace of implementation. Such actions have no doubt confounded the worsening socioeconomic conditions in Zambia today.

Conclusion

This chapter shows clearly that the institutions and processes of policymaking in Zambia have undergone rapid transformation. The public policy environment of the 1980s and 1990s is radically different from that of the 1960s and early 1970s. The 1980s were characterized and propelled by a deep and prolonged economic crisis, which has so far proved intractable. The 1990s will be characterized by political instability and further economic challenges as democratic regimes struggle to survive.

The well-adapted institutional arrangements for policymaking and implementation that have been put in place in Zambia can only bear fruit and be sustained if they can contend with the following factors. The inertia and lack of commitment to policy and program implementation on the part of both political and technocratic personnel must be overcome. The issue of inadequate funding and other relevant resources, or delays and hitches in the cash flow for project activities, must be addressed. Attention also must be given to the problems of ineffective and poor management and support services and the absence of support for systematic training, not only of policy formulators and executors but the entire spectrum of system personnel. Finally, policymakers must address the problem of inadequate information flows for timely feedback and readjustment in the policy process.

Notes

1. Sources used in the preparation of this chapter include: M. C. Bwalya, "Policy Teaching at the National Institute of Public Administration," *AMTIESA* [Association of Management Training Institutes for Eastern and Southern Africa] *Bulletin*, vol. 3, no. 1 (1991), pp. 2–6; K. D. Kaunda, *Humanism in Zambia and a Guide to Its Implementation, Parts 1 and 2* (Lusaka: Government Printer, 1967 and 1974); G. F. Lungu, "Citizen Participation in Zambia Development Administration: A Critical Appraisal of the Development Committees," *Africanus*, vol. 17, no. 112 (1987), pp. 5–20; S. A. Quick, "Bureaucracy and Rural Socialism in Zambia," *Journal of Modern African Studies*, vol. 15, no. 3 (1977), pp. 379–400; and *Politics in Zambia*, ed. William Tordoff (Manchester: Manchester University Press, 1974).

2. On October 31, 1991, Kenneth Kaunda was defeated in a landslide victory by the Movement for Multiparty Democracy (MMD), led by Frederick Chiluba. Kenneth Kaunda had been ruling Zambia since 1964. Zambia became a one-party state in 1973. For a detailed discussion of Zambian politics, see Munyonzwe Hamalengwa, *Class Struggles in Zambia, 1889–1989 and the Fall of Kenneth Kaunda, 1990–1991* (New York: University Press of America, 1992).

3. *United National Independence Party Constitution*, as amended at the party conference held at Mulungushi Rock, Kabwe, Zambia, August 18, 1988, p. 8.

4. Ibid.

5. Kaunda drew on the idea of African humanism, a communal approach to social welfare, which he claimed was a pillar of strength in

precolonial society. Humanism was contrasted with the individualistic approach of capitalism. In practice, humanism came to refer to Zambia's state-centered socialism.

6. *United National Independence Party Constitution,* Article 53.

7. Headed by a director general (at the level of a senior permanent secretary).

8. The bureaucratical model is characterized by a hierarchy with specialization of tasks; considerable centralization of decisionmaking power; reliance on formal rules, regulations, and procedures; and appointments based on qualifications, career service, and impersonality. The structure of the technocratic bodies emphasized the concepts of rationality and efficiency in the implementation of party policies and programs.

9. It must be noted here that before the fourth national development plan, the party and government relied on external experts for policy analysis on the pretext that there was no local expertise.

10. More specifically, a concern with finding combinations with a greater probability of maximizing outputs from limited available resources.

11. See *Times of Zambia,* November 3, 1968, p. 1, and *Zambia Daily Mail,* November 3, 1988, p. 1.

12. Of chairmen of subcommittees of the Central Committee of the party.

13. Patrick E. Ollawa, *Participatory Democracy in Zambia: The Political Economy of National Development* (Devon: Arthur Stockwell, 1979).

5

Tanzania: Moving Beyond the One-Party State

Rwekaza S. Mukandala & William Shellukindo

It is now recognized that policymaking involves choice, but it is also true that the process of making choices has received limited attention from Africans and Africanists alike. Much has been said and written about the rights of African states to make their own decisions and policies. These rights have been regarded as a sine qua non for real sovereignty. Within the African domestic policymaking arena, much also has been said about which institutions are supreme in decisionmaking. These institutions have ranged from the party to the military. Yet, there has been little concrete research and discourse on the actual process of decisionmaking, the actions involved, their impact, and implications for sustainability.

Decisionmaking and the Policy Process in Tanzania

To fully appreciate Tanzania's decisionmaking and policy process we must consider both its formal and its practical dimensions as well as the important issue of actors.

Formal Policymaking Decision Structures

Tanzania's constitution, like similar documents elsewhere "sets out *the framework* and the *principal functions* of the organs of government of a state, and declares the principles governing the operation of those organs."[1] Shivji correctly refers to the constitution as the *grundnorm*[2] and the basic norm.[3] The constitution defines, describes, and sanctions the laws and distribution of policymaking authority in the nation-state. The constitution also spells out the hierarchy of power and authority relationships, defines the relationships, and describes the functioning of the various state organs and their responsibilities and limitations regarding policymaking.[4]

The dominant political ideology is also an important formal structural feature of policymaking in Tanzania. Since 1967 and until very recently, the ideology of Ujamaa or socialism and self-reliance has been an important factor that has formed the background for almost all policy decisions. The ideology spelled out the ends to be sought and the means to those ends. It also spelled out preconditions that had to be met before one becomes an important actor in the policy arena.[5]

Tanzania's constitution and ideology established the rules of the game, defined what was legal and acceptable, propounded the important characteristics of the political and policymaking system, and established the general parameters within which policies were made. These two features were also relatively stable and have been a result of the nature of developments in other important spheres of the political system, including struggles within and over the state.

According to the Tanzanian constitution of 1977, the sole political party, Chama Cha Mapinduzi (CCM), is "the final authority in respect of all matters" in Tanzania.[6] Between 1965, when Tanzania became a one-party state, and 1977, when the constitution was enacted, the leading role and final say on "all matters" did not derive from the constitution. The party simply asserted its leadership.[7] It was only in 1977 that the party's leading role was constitutionally provided. The party's policymaking structures ranged from the party chairman, who currently is also president of the United Republic, through the Central Committee, the National Executive Committee (NEC), and the party general conference, which is held every five years. The party's policymaking and administrative functions[8] are coordinated by a secretariat. Top leaders of the party are also members of the cabinet as ministers without portfolio. According to CCM, "the party guides the Government and its organs by first of all setting the goals and objectives, policies, directives, and frequent orders, which are then transformed by the Government into plans of action and laws."[9]

Next in the formal structure is the government, which is headed by the president, in whom all executive powers relating to the union are vested.[10] The president is assisted by a cabinet appointed in consultation with the prime minister of his choice. The public sector is organized around a ministerial system, but includes independent departments like the Civil Service Department in the Office of the President; commissions, which include the Civil

Service Commission; and standing committees, such as the Standing Committee on Parastatal Organizations.

According to the constitution and the party, the role of government in policy decisionmaking is the transformation of policy decisions of the party into plans of action and laws. According to the formal design, the party decides and the government implements or decides on implementation. Thus, the party pronounces on basic policy, with the government deciding on operational policy. This is the conception that informed Goran Hyden's seminal paper on policymaking in Tanzania.[11]

The Practice of Policymaking

In practice, demands and needs from the public entered the policy process through both party and government structures. Government ministries initiated policy in response to public needs and demands manifested through field workers, the mass media, parliament, or citizens. As Shellukindo has pointed out:

> When a problem has been identified in a certain Ministry or field of work, the Ministry responsible usually initiates the policy process by preparing policy proposals in the form of a "Draft Cabinet Paper." The Draft policy proposals are then circulated to other Ministries and independent departments. The next stage is a final draft for discussion by Permanent/Principal Secretaries. The government has established an Inter-Ministerial Technical Committee (IMTC) comprising all the Principal Secretaries. This is the intermediate stage where policy recommendations are firmed-up.[12]

As the paper further explains, depending on the opinion of the IMTC a go-ahead may be given for the ministry concerned to prepare a cabinet paper requesting a policy decision at cabinet level, which may lead to the enactment of a law. There are also occasions when policy proposals are referred to the initiators for recasting. There are also instances when a proposal is turned down at the IMTC level. For a turned-down draft cabinet paper, the ministry responsible is normally advised to solve the real or assumed problem using existing mechanisms.[13]

It must be emphasized that the above process involved not only secondary or operational policy, but also principal or basic issues. Because such issues may be involved, the party was represented in the cabinet by its chairman, vice-chairman, and secretary-general. The chairman was, of course, also the president. The other two were ministers without portfolio.

The party also initiated policy through its own structures. The party secretariat and its various committees could research policy and forward the results to the Central Committee and, ultimately, the NEC for decision. Party branches and other organs at the district and regional level could also express needs and/or demands, which could then be channeled upward in the party structure for processing and decision, although this was rare.

A majority of Tanzania's key policies were decided upon by the NEC. Decisions were based on submissions of the party secretariat endorsed by the Central Committee. At times, decisions were based on submissions of the party chairman. Such policy decisions include the Arusha Declaration (1967); "Politics Is Agriculture" (1972); "Agriculture: Life or Death" (1974); the dissolution of cooperative unions (1976); and the Musoma Resolution on Education (1974). The power of the NEC reflects its central role in governance in Tanzania, particularly during the years when Julius Nyerere was president.

It also must be pointed out that, given the structures mentioned above, there was little pressure-group activity regarding public policy until recently. There were few independent associations in civil society, and those that did exist treaded carefully when it came to anything resembling pressure on the party-state. The few official organizations, such as the party-affiliated trade unions, were meek and hesitant. Institutions of higher learning remain few, although they have at times offered considerable criticism and have contributed to the policy process. The lack of think tanks and seasoned public policy analysts and commentators is also a debilitating factor. Many of the pressure groups are issue oriented and deal with local issues rather than national concerns. Their occasional involvement in national issues has been rarely appreciated, as university students found out in April/May 1990.[14]

The mass media have played a role in the policy process, but their data have sometimes been unreliable and their analysis superficial. Their preoccupation with what is "newsworthy" has tilted the focus in favor of personalities rather than issues, and even sensationalism rather than objectivity. On the other hand, the media have sensitized policymakers to problems or potential problems requiring their attention.

Overall, there was a serious gap between what the policy process was supposed to be, and what it was in reality. Party supremacy was more apparent than real. The above scenario proved difficult to realize in practice and was the result of several incongruencies. First, there developed a misfit between the perceived policy role of the party and its policy decisionmaking capacity. The party suffered from a serious dearth of talent in policy and other related fields. Most party officials had little education, let alone the kind of sophisticated skills necessary for policy analysis.

Second, the secondary role defined for government in policymaking did not match the resources in personnel, structures and systems, and finances available to the government. Third, there was a misfit between the self-declared commitment, dedication, and competence of the party in policymaking, and the failure of some of its self-declared policies in practice. Party policies that did not work include the policy on education (Musoma Resolution of 1975); the trade policy (Operation Maduka, 1976); the policy on Cooperative Unions and Local Authorities (1972–1976); and the policy on irrigation (Iringa Declaration).

The fourth factor is the incongruence between what Nyerere has called the "trappings of independence"[15] on the one hand, and the realities of the power of the international capitalist system of which Tanzania is a part. Tanzania's dependency on international institutions for goods, markets, services, technology, skills, and finances has been a major constraint on the formal machinery of policymaking. The inability to meet its needs from readily available domestic resources hindered many policy objectives, especially given the nature of the goals that the party wanted realized, including a frontal transformation and modernization of the country's economy and society. These are huge and complex goals that have eluded even those countries that are better endowed in resources, leadership, implementation capacity, and historical circumstances.

Redefining Decisionmaking Structures and Processes

In the 1980s, there were changes in government structures, party structures, and in the policy relationship between government and party in Tanzania. All of these changes were responses to past failures, confusion, ineffectiveness, and even conflict in policymaking. The winds of liberalization and multi-partyism have brought in even more profound changes since 1987.

Changes in Government Structures

The changes in government structures centered around the ministries and the cabinet. Before 1982, the cabinet secretariat consisted of a secretary of the cabinet and a clerk to the cabinet. In 1982, a cabinet secretariat of four cabinet coordinators, one clerk, and one deputy clerk was established. In 1984, a system of cabinet under secretaries was established. These represented the professions involved in policymaking, especially political scientists and administrators, economists, financial analysts, lawyers, and foreign service officials. Presently, the cabinet secretariat has an establishment of thirteen professionals. The Inter-Ministerial Technical Committee (whose functions were described above) was also established at this time. A cadre of private secretaries was also formed to assist ministers and regional commissioners in their policymaking functions. Policy units are currently being established in each ministry to strengthen the policy analysis functions. Finally, cabinet liaison officials have now been appointed for each ministry to improve policy dialogue, coordination, and analysis between ministries and the cabinet secretariat.

Political changes associated with the introduction of multi-partyism have been accompanied by the depoliticization of the state bureaucracy. The civil service can no longer be involved in partisan politics, although its members retain their civic and political rights.

Changes in Party Structure

The party also made structural changes to maximize effectiveness and efficiency. At its Congress in 1982, the party expanded and consolidated its secretariat through a number of measures: creating more organizational units or departments; appointing members of the Central Committee to head the departments of the NEC; reestablishing the post of secretary-general of the party, which had been abolished in 1967; and, finally, appointing an overall secretary to the party NEC. The party secretary-general was now in charge of all party affairs. Second, the size of the Central Committee was reduced from forty members to eighteen to facilitate deci-sionmaking, and the Central Committee began to function as a politburo.

The whirlwind of changes brought about by calls for liber-alization and multiparty democracy resulted in further changes in the party and to the party system. The Eighth Amendment to the Constitution[16] removed relevant sections in the constitution that gave the party monopoly control of the political space in the country. It also removed party supremacy in policymaking; other acts freed local authorities from party control. The drying up of government subsidies to the party also resulted in belt-tightening measures. These measures included the firing of more than one-third of party employees; the closure of almost all ideological training colleges; and the reduction of departments and commissions. Some of the party functionaries, including party chairpersons at all levels, now work on a voluntary basis. The pomp and pageantry are also gone, including a police escort for the party secretary-general and special license plates for party cars and trucks. All party branch offices at places of work have also been closed, and the party's women and youth organization affiliates have been banished from work places. Finally, party representatives are no longer a permanent fixture on decisionmaking bodies such as the boards of directors of public enterprises.

Changes in the Relationship of Government and Party

The respective roles of government and party in policymaking as formally defined in the constitution have been hard to realize in practice. In response to policy-related problems, the late Prime Minister Edward M. Sokoine issued *Prime Ministerial Circular Number 1 of 1984,* which among other things redefined the concepts of basic or principal policy and secondary or operational policy. The former was confined to political decisions that sought "major changes" and involved high-level decisionmaking.[17] All substantive policy issues were left to the normal government machinery. Second, it was put on record that government through its ministries could initiate "basic policy." All that had to be done was to seek the blessing of the party before implementation. The above changes, among others, formally reinstated the bureaucracy in its traditional policymaking role.

As the economic crisis of the 1980s intensified and Tanzania moved closer to the IMF and World Bank, party dominance in policymaking continued to wane in favor of government. Personnel from multilateral lending agencies were more likely to talk to fellow technocrats in the government ministries, banks, and public enterprises than with politicians. As the 1980s progressed the party increasingly reigned rather than ruled over the policy process. The party rubber-stamped agreements already reached, diplomatically airing disagreements where policy choices were unacceptable. In effect, the party role was reduced to watching from the sidelines as government professionals and technocrats took direction from the international lending agencies.

The introduction of multi-partyism has formalized the above arrangements. As noted, the Eighth Amendment to the Constitution in 1992 abolished the supremacy and the political monopoly of the sole political party. Additional legislation provided for the formation of political parties and the separation of party activities from government activities.[18] Parties can now deliberate and formulate policies, and if elected to power, they can oversee policy implementation by the bureaucracy.

Institutional Implication of Sustainability

In the past, policymaking as described above rarely took institutional implications into consideration at the policy formulation stage. This omission was a result of several factors. The very nature of policymaking, formally dominated by the party but in practice a domain of the bureaucracy, had many unintended consequences. Devoid of a capacity for effective policy analysis, the party proceeded to make policy pronouncements with little analytical backing. This practice was accompanied by a tendency to ignore and denigrate technical and professional advice, especially from the bureaucracy.

Government was also not above blame. The capacity for policy analysis, research, and review has been totally lacking in some of the ministries. Policies were never revised unless there was a crisis or some important people were affected. There was no systematic evaluation of policy and no clear understanding and appreciation of the importance of policy analysis. Senior officials confused policy analysis with the planning of projects. Until recently, there was no institutional policy analysis framework at the ministerial level. It is only recently that policy analysis as a discrete activity has been established. As a consequence of past practices, policy reversal was very difficult and policy termination almost out of the question, even when evidence existed of institutional incapacity or bottlenecks.

In cases where institutional shortcomings could no longer be ignored, policy change was lengthy and difficult. For example, the shortcomings of the Civil Service Act of 1962 were realized in 1981, but it was not until 1989 that changes were finally effected. In another instance, crop authorities swindled peasants and accumulated huge bank overdrafts for a decade beginning in 1976 before structural changes were introduced in agricultural marketing during the period 1985–1986. The following three additional factors have been consistently overlooked during the policy formulation stage.

Finances. Rarely have adequate costing and other financial implications of proposed policies been worked out. Presumably the underlying assumptions were that a donor could be secured, contributions could be collected from the people, or taxes could be raised. Ideology may also have had something to do with this nonchalant attitude toward money. The Arusha Declaration decreed that "money is not the basis of development."[19] Such thinking and practices have had serious consequences for the sustainability of projects. In particular, little attention has been given to costing and budgeting for maintenance. Once a road or building project was completed, for example, budget allocations for maintenance were never a serious concern, and rapid deterioration inevitably occurred. The poor state of roads in the country is a result of this tendency.

Human resource development. Many aspects of human resource development were also not taken into account. The numbers, quality, and motivation of personnel were more often than not overlooked. The Civil Service Census of 1988, for example, illustrates this tendency. The census counted the number of people in office by establishment, but gave no information about their skill levels. No judgments were made about the level of education, the value system in place, or the appropriateness of job placement within the civil service system.

Policy linkages. Policy linkages have not always been fully appreciated. The party tended to pronounce policy without consulting government. Government was regarded purely as an implementing organ. Within government, ministries tended to initiate sectoral policies without consultation with other ministries. For example, many industrial projects were initiated by the Ministry of Industry without assuring adequate power supply through consultations with the Ministry of Energy and the power supply company. Musoma Textiles, Mwanza Textiles, and the spinning and weaving mills at Tabora all fell victim to the above omission. In another instance, cashew nut–processing capacity was being expanded through the construction of new factories when cashew nut production was declining. Liaison with the Ministry of Agriculture could have resulted in a change of policy. Finally, a starch-processing factory was put into operation in Shinyanga without first securing assurances of adequate supplies of the raw material cassava from the concerned ministry.

The importance of sound policy analysis and development management has been realized only recently, and were a result of internal self-criticism and evaluation following past problems and inadequacies. Gradually, public policy actors in Tanzania have realized the need for change. Even before the current changes the party had recognized that policy analysis did not hurt, and if anything, minimized the likelihood of failure. It also recognized that sound policy analysis "provides standards of argument and an intellectual structure for public discourse."[20] The government bureaucracy also came to realize the importance of planning and structuring for policy analysis and coordination. The above changes in orientation were also partly a result of pressures from international finance institutions.

Consultation and Policy Sustainability

The issue of consultation needs to be discussed at two levels: government functionaries and government clients. Efforts have been made to maximize the participation of the civil service in policymaking. The creation of a cabinet secretariat; the formation of the IMTC to which various experts can be invited by relevant principal secretaries; the creation of cabinet liaison officers; and the redefinition of basic and secondary policy have all increased bureaucratic participation in the policy process.

It is at the level of policy recipients, the clients of public organizations, that problems remain. The absence of interest groups has been an important factor. Moreover, lack of appreciation for the efforts of the few groups that do exist has not been encouraging. The nature of Parliament, especially its structural characteristic as a committee of the party, and the low number of members of Parliament who are elected rather than appointed, have constrained Parliament's function as a mouthpiece of policy recipients. Changes have now been introduced to remove the first constraint. The number of parliamentarians directly elected by constituencies is bound to increase in the next Parliament. State-party control of the media (press and radio) has also hindered the policy process, but some change has been occurring, with several papers now published by private groups, although the radio remains under state control.

What needs to be emphasized is the negative consequences of lack of consultation. It cannot be denied that it has had financial, human, and even political consequences. The issue of the head tax can be used for illustrative purposes. A bill was introduced in Parliament mandating the taxation of every citizen over seventeen years in Tanzania. Unlike the colonial hut tax, which, in practice, taxed men as owners/heads of households, the head tax included women. Although the gender issue was raised with regard to the head tax by some members of Parliament and some councils, it was brushed aside.

In practice, the law contravenes one of the basic cultural norms of several groups in Tanzania whereby women are not supposed to interact with outsiders. The interaction between tax collectors and women has at times been an infringement of that norm and has not been looked on favorably by some of the societies concerned. As a consequence, not only have the taxes not been paid, but bitterness and alienation have also accompanied attempts to collect the tax. Had there been meaningful consultation, many of these difficulties could have been avoided.

Policy Capacity and Human Resources

Many of Tanzania's senior policymakers are either unaware of or lack a broad conception and appreciation of public policy management. Many are from the professions and have not had the benefits of an orientation into the broader issues of governance.

It must also be pointed out that although most Tanzanians have had access to formal education, only 5.6 percent are educated above the secondary level and 67 percent possess only a basic education. Moreover, few of the educated have had opportunities for continuous training and retooling. There has also been little orientation for senior officials assuming new positions. For example, the top executive training program has placed little emphasis on policy analysis and management issues. Thus, old habits have continued unchecked.

Changes in methods of recruitment into the civil service have not been helpful. The adoption of the system of allocating university graduates into positions in the civil service without the benefit of interviews, personnel assessment, and a selection process has brought unqualified people into the bureaucracy. A system of appointing people to senior positions that disregards experience and age has had adverse effects. As a result, inexperienced persons have assumed top positions without learning and knowing how to manage and coordinate complex ministerial responsibilities. The combination of youth and inexperience has also produced a tendency to stay too long (until retirement), thus perpetuating a level of incompetence. On the other hand, some personnel leave government after a short time to complete their education abroad, disrupting the smooth operation of the organization.

External Actors and Internal Capacity Building

There is no question that external actors continue to play an important role in Tanzania given international structural realities. The economic crisis of the last decade has expanded their role even further.

Interviews with many senior policymakers reveal several interesting points. First is their conviction that sustainable policy changes are those initiated from within the country, albeit with donor assistance. Recipient-driven programs have a greater chance of sustainability than donor-driven initiatives. Second, there is a concern that many donor initiatives lack analysis of what is on the ground. Consequently, there is a noted tendency to impose new programs even where similar initiatives are already in place. Third, the recipient's capacity to change or to internalize change has not been fully analyzed or appreciated. Finally, there has been an overemphasis on spending or, in donors' parlance, "moving money," a practice which many LDC policymakers find wasteful. All of the above have contributed to a resentment of donor involvement in policymaking.

What appears to be preferred is the institutionalization of mutually agreed upon procedures that would give due weight to recipient realities, resources, and sovereignty. Donor involvement through funding technical support, supplying machinery and equipment, and providing training and research can only contribute to sustainable capacity when recipient realities are fully taken into account. See Chapter 9 for further discussion of this issue.

Conclusion

This chapter has attempted to describe and analyze the policymaking structures, processes, and actors in Tanzania. It has been pointed out that there was a divergence between what was mandated by law and ideology on the one hand, and what in practice constituted policymaking in Tanzania. It has been shown that steps were taken during the 1980s to bridge that gap.

The chapter has also focused on the institutional changes that have been initiated in light of past policymaking inadequacies, bottlenecks, and even failures. These changes have occurred in government structures, party structures, and in the relationship between the two. The question of actor consultation has also been discussed. Although measures to enhance consultation between and within the party and the state have been taken, the same cannot be said about consulting with the clients of public organizations: civil society. There remains a serious lack of consultative mechanisms through which societal groups can effectively communicate with government. It has also been pointed out that several aspects of human resource development still require attention. Finally, international donor participation in developing country public policymaking, implementation, and evaluation has increased during the 1980s. More efforts need to be made, however, to rationalize and channel donor involvement toward the creation of self-sustaining public policy capacity.

Notes

The authors wich to acknowledge the helpful comments and criticisms made by Joseph Rugumyamheto, director, Policy Analysis, Research and

Review, Civil Service Department, Government of Tanzania.

1. I. Shivji, *The Legal Foundations of the Union in Tanzania's Union and Zanzibar Constitutions* (Dar es Salaam: Dar es Salaam University Press, 1990), pp. 8–9.

2. Ibid. For example, ground law or fundamental law.

3. Ibid.

4. Ibid.

5. Such as politicians divesting themselves from property and investments that might influence their policy choices, or the mandate that civil servants not be allowed to own rental property.

6. *The Constitution of the United Republic of Tanzania 1977* (Dar es Salaam: Government Printer, 1990).

7. In 1992, Tanzania changed to a multiparty political system.

8. Since 1967, political officers from the party have headed Tanzania's regional and district administrations.

9. *Mwongozo wa CCM* (Dar es Salaam: Government Printer, 1981), p. 103.

10. *The Constitution of 1977*, Section 34. Union matters include the constitution and the government of the United Republic, external affairs, defense and security policy, emergency powers, citizenship, immigration, external trade and borrowing, the public service, income tax, harbors, aid, transport, posts and telecommunications, currency, coinage and legal tender, banks, industrial licensing, and statistics. Nonunion matters include education, internal trade, health, and so on.

11. Goran Hyden, "We Must Run While Others Walk: Policy–making for Socialist Development in Tanzania-Type of Politics," in *Papers on the Political Economy of Tanzania*, ed. Kwan S. Kim, Robert B. Mabele, and Michael J. Schultheis. (London: Heineman Educational Books, 1979), pp. 5–13. See also G. Munishi, "Policymaking and Implementation in the Social Services Sector," in *Conflicts on Structural Adjustment*, ed. G. W. Strom (London: Macmillan, 1991); Rwekaza S. Mukandala, "Bureaucracy and Agricultural Policy: The Case of Tanzania," in *Bureaucracy and Developmental Policies in the Third World*, ed. H. K. Asmerom, R. Hoppe, and R. B. Jain (Amsterdam: Vu University Press, 1992), pp. 60–74.

12. William Shellukindo, "Enhancing Public Policy Management Capacity in Africa: Issues and Critical Skills" (Dar es Salaam, mimeo, 1989).

13. Ibid.

14. Students at the University of Dar es Salaam went on strike in April 1990, demanding among other things an increase in the education budget, necessary repairs to the university building and other infrastructure, increased salaries for university lecturers, closure of the city waste dump located in a heavily populated neighborhood, explanation and accountability from those responsible for burning down the Bank of Tanzania building in 1988, and so on. The government responded by closing down the university for more than one year.

15. J. K. Nyerere, "The Process of Liberation," in *Politics and State in the Third World*, ed. Harry Goulbourne (London: Macmillan Press Limited, 1979), pp. 248–258.

16. United Republic of Tanzania, Eighth Amendment to the Constitution, 1992.

17. According to the principal secretary, Office of the Prime Minister, Government Minute, 1991.

18. See, in particular, United Republic of Tanzania, Act No. 5, 1992.

19. Julius Nyerere, *Ujamaa Essays on Socialism* (Dar es Salaam and New York: Oxford University Press, 1968).
20. G. Majone, *Evidence, Argument, and Persuasion in the Policy Process* (New Haven, Conn.: Yale University Press, 1989), p. 7.

6

Kenya: Contextual Factors and the Policy Process

Walter O. Oyugi

This chapter presents a broad perspective of the context and manner in which public policy formulation and implementation occur in Kenya. The point of departure is a brief statement on the sociocultural factors influencing the policy process.

The Sociopolitical and Economic Setting

As Bauer and Gergen[1] have pointed out, policymaking is the setting of courses of action designed to implement the values, usually of a fairly large group of persons, on a given issue without unduly compromising other values on other issues. If we accept this position, then the social, political, and economic setting within which the process takes place has direct bearing on the policy made. The demands to which the policymakers respond usually originate in the society, and it is that environment that places limits and constraints upon what can be done by those charged with the task of policymaking.[2] Often the policy agenda (that is, what should be acted upon) is also influenced by the dynamics within that environment.

It is my contention that social, political, and economic conditions in Kenya directly influence agenda setting as well as the actual formulation of public policies. At the social level, the value orientation of many Kenyans, which influences them to react to policies and their impact in ethnic terms, is often a major consideration in both agenda setting and actual policy formulation.

Policies affect people directly or indirectly. In Kenya, society continues to be predominantly organized geographically, according to ethnic group identities. Policies relating to the development of certain areas are, *ipso facto,* policies that affect a given ethnic group directly. The criterion of social equity has therefore been a consideration, given the nature of the social structure of the society.

At the political level, the roles that each of the legally authorized political organs (the executive, the legislature, and the ruling party) of the state play in policymaking varies. Over the years, the executive has emerged as the center of policy initiative and also as the center of agenda determination. The political arms of the executive are the president and his cabinet. By law and convention, the cabinet under the leadership of the president is responsible for policy approval regarding both substance and timing. The executive also works through the civil bureaucracy. Both the strengths and weaknesses of the bureaucracy in policy analysis bear directly on the quality of policies formulated and implemented.

The legislative role in policymaking has been primarily reactive. This characteristic is partly due to the structural inhibitions inherited at independence. The Westminster model of government that Kenya inherited was modified when the nation became a republic, but the procedures associated with it in the passage of bills remains unchanged. More important, the initiative on the policy front remains with the president and his cabinet. The role the legislature plays is therefore limited because it cannot meaningfully participate in setting a policy agenda. The 1993 convening of a multiparty Parliament after controversial elections is not likely to change this.

The structural configuration of Kenya's parliament is also a major constraint. Parliamentarians lack the requisite facilities necessary for the satisfactory discharge of legislative duties, namely, a well-developed library with up-to-date material, a support staff to assist in the preparation of policy papers, and adequate office space. Furthermore, there are no standing functional committees that can routinely subpoena government officers and/or relevant public officials to testify on major policy issues.

The political environment has also imposed constraints on parliamentary autonomy in decisionmaking. The emergence of "court" politics under Mzee Jomo Kenyatta[3] (1963–1975) fundamentally reduced the influence of parliamentarians in the legislative process. As a result, the Parliament was increasingly required to simply endorse decisions already made by the "court" actors. The dominance of the political executive and the systematic patronage culture that accompanied it meant that only those parliamentarians perceived to be supportive of the regime benefited from the system. This style of politics had the effect of taming

Parliament, effectively reducing its voice on legislative matters.

The relationship between the political executive and the Parliament during Daniel T. arap Moi's regime (the period of the de facto one-party state, 1978–1992) did not change for the better. If anything, executive dominance continued, and Moi's interventionist style ensured that there would be no doubt about the thinking of the executive on the issues of the moment. Indeed, Moi's preemptive decisionmaking style often put other policy actors on the defensive and deprived them of the initiative.

However, the relative strength of the Kenya Parliament in contrast with those of other Third World countries (other than India) should also be emphasized. Over the years the Kenyan Parliament has had a group of very active backbenchers who have, whenever opportunities arose, seriously scrutinized policies initiated by the executive.

There have also been many instances in which individual backbenchers have initiated legislation on their own through private member bills. Often these were rejected by the front bench, only to reappear later in modified form as government bills. Therefore, one cannot deny that backbenchers have sometimes had a direct role to play in policymaking in Kenya. Indeed, there are a few cases where as a result of individual member initiatives, bills were drafted and subsequently accepted and implemented by the government. For instance, the practices of hire-purchase and paying married women house allowances were the result of private member bills. What is important to note, however, is that nothing can be achieved by Parliament if the political executive opposes the measure.

If the role of Parliament in policymaking has been marginal, that of the ruling party, the Kenya African National Union (KANU) (1963–1992) has been even more dismal. There is no evidence to show that KANU has been a key actor in the policymaking process. As David Leonard correctly observed, the Kenyatta years produced an administrative state, where bureaucrats rather than politicians made most of the day-to-day decisions.[4] The emergence of such a state of affairs subordinated the political party to the executive, giving the party no voice in policy matters.[5]

The efforts of the Moi regime to breathe some life into KANU had little, if any, effect on its operation. The changes worth mentioning occurred in 1989 when a decision was made to strengthen the administrative capacity of the party by creating new administrative units in the party secretariat, headed by party-appointed directors. The action was taken in recognition of the fact that the party lacked an internal organizational framework through which it could influence policy. The absence of a well-developed and staffed secretariat had been a major missing link since the inception of the party in 1960.

Even after the strengthening of the secretariat in 1989, not much was heard from the party on matters of policy formulation. As it later turned out, the directors did not have much to do. No attempt was made to synchronize their roles with relevant departments in the central bureaucracy. For instance, the director of legal affairs did not know how his activities related to those of the attorney general. The same absence of knowledge was also evident in the attorney general's office with regard to the activities of the director's office and of the director of youth and women affairs vis-à-vis her counterparts in the Ministry of Culture and Social Services. Others operated similarly. In the process of trying to justify their positions, some directors tried to preempt certain roles for their units or departments, only to run into problems that eventually led to the dismantling of most of the newly created units in May 1991 and the dismissal of the directors.

The state was not prepared to have the party intrude upon its traditional operational domain.[6] Apparently there was no will on the part of the political executive, who was also the head of KANU, to change the nature of the relationship between the executive and the party on matters of public policy formulation. Thus, KANU remained a peripheral actor in the policy formulation process throughout the time it existed as the state party (1963–1992) and before the reemergence of a multiparty system.

An analysis of the institutional context of policy formulation in Kenya must also focus on private sector institutions (including NGOs), considering the important role that they play in national development. Indeed, their role is underscored in the current National Development Plan (1989–1993), which notes that the plan "will rely a great deal on growth initiatives from the private sector."[7]

Kenya also depends on external sources in financing budget deficits and for general investment, with dependence on external support increasing steadily. For instance, external public debt outstanding from 1980 to 1987 grew from K£0.7 to K£3.8 billion, representing a rise from 32 percent to 62 percent of GDP at factor cost.[8]

Overall, domestic private and nongovernmental institutions as well as external institutions exercise significant influence on monetary and related development policies because of their financial leverage over the state.

Several instruments of influence are at work. One such instrument, especially in the field of development policy, is that of technical assistance. The ideas and values of donor-originated technical assistance have directly influenced the nature and character of most of the development policies that Kenya has been associated with since independence.[9] Foreign investors, through local agents of various transnationals, also seek on a regular basis to influence the policy process. Their influence is expressed in both informal (for example, through personal contacts) and formal channels (for example, through interest group activity, including the Kenya Association of Manufacturers, Federation of Kenya Employers, and the Kenya Chamber of Commerce and Industry).

The influence of interest groups on public policy decisionmaking has been on the increase, especially since 1971 when civil servants were officially allowed to engage in private business.[10] The result has been the overlapping presence of many senior civil servants (the policymakers) in both public and private sector organizations. This overlapping membership and interest is what has provided for the informality with which some policy decisions are made.

The foregoing discussion suggests that the donor community and the private sector have had more influence on policy formulation in Kenya than has the Parliament and the ruling party (KANU) and that the civil bureaucracy with the support of the presidency has been the major actor. This overview of the policy process has also shown the extent to which various contextual factors influence and often control the process. A better understanding of the institutional context of policymaking in Kenya can be gained if some tangible policies are isolated and analyzed. That is the main task of the remainder of the chapter.

The Formulation of Macropolicies

The distinction drawn between the formulation of macropolicies and sectoral policies is analytical and, therefore, somewhat artificial. However, the distinction is made simply to indicate that there are some policies that by their nature require the involvement of the more manifestly political institutions or actors. Policies on development goals, the economy, national development strategy, and so on fall within this category.

A closer examination of some existing policies suggests that the involvement by political institutions has not been fully achieved. A case in point is the formulation of the broad national development goals and policies contained in the 1965 *Sessional Paper* on African socialism.[11] These policies and goals have guided Kenya's development efforts since independence. Some important tenets of the document include: egalitarianism as a major development goal, the concept of regional balance in pursuing development strategies, and the principle of a mixed economy. However, the ruling party as such had no direct involvement in the preparation of the paper. Rather, the document was prepared by a few senior civil servants working closely with an expatriate adviser. Once approval was obtained at the appropriate level of government, it was then presented to Parliament as a sessional paper. The document generated a lot of debate in Parliament, but none of the policy recommendations were changed as a result of the debate.[12] It is important to stress again that this document, which Kenyatta once referred to as Kenya's development bible and which continued to be regarded as such in the Moi regime, was produced with no input from the ruling party and Parliament.

The broad goals and policies contained in the 1965 *Sessional Paper* can be found in all the national development plans produced since then. As with the preparation of sessional papers, the national development plans have never been presented to the ruling party for discussion and appraisal. In the case of Parliament, the development plans have been presented as finished products intended for general information of the parliamentarians.

The general and specific policies that find expression in the development plans are originated by individual government ministries, working in close collaboration with the Ministry of Planning and National Development. Sectoral and intersectoral working committees set up to generate ideas on specific policies for a given plan are exclusively made up of civil servants and their expatriate colleagues scattered throughout the various ministries. On some occasions, local academicians have been coopted into the committees. Committee recommendations are usually discussed in-house by an expanded committee of the same people, with no effort made to involve outsiders. In the end, what comes out as the national development plan for a given period is a document that reflects the values and priorities of the civil service and the donor community.

Another important ideological policy document that was produced by the government and contained broad, national development values, goals, and strategies is the 1986 *Sessional Paper* on economic management, which articulated privatization and other structural adjustment measures.[13] Like the 1965 paper, this document was the brainchild of senior bureaucrats and their expatriate advisers, especially in the Ministry of Planning and National Development. Having received formal approval at the appropriate level in government, the document was also presented to Parliament as a sessional paper and was endorsed intact.

As noted, the examples cited also had substantial involvement by the donor community through their locally based staff. Therefore, whatever mistakes have been made in the policymaking process, expatriate input can be viewed as part and parcel of the problem. Indeed, a recent World Bank document observed that to the extent that international donor agencies have been deeply involved in the development efforts in Africa since independence, they cannot escape part of the blame for the African economic crises today.[14]

The party manifestos produced between elections have also been sources of broad development values. They, too, have lacked input from the relevant party organs before they have been published. On some occasions, the authors have been civil servants. It is interesting to note that this essentially KANU-style of manifesto preparation has been emulated by the new political parties that have emerged in the multiparty era in Kenya. For instance, none of the major opposition parties that produced an election manifesto subjected the document to any open discussion by party supporters or their representatives. Some parties even acknowledged the authors of the document, an indication that the ideas contained in the document were of limited origin.

The picture that emerges is that the formulation of macro-policies in Kenya has been dominated by the civil bureaucracy acting in collaboration with donor representatives and supported by the political executive (that is, the presidency).[15]

Sectoral Policies

In the formulation of sectoral policies, two approaches have been institutionalized in Kenya: (1) sectoral working committees; and (2) presidential committees or commissions on selected problems or issues. What appears to be a third approach has emerged in the last decade and involves a more open, participatory approach to policymaking.

The Sectoral Working Group Approach

Development planning is a major source of national development policies. At independence, Kenya inherited a weak planning system based on ad hoc committees, which dissolved as soon as a public sector investment plan had been prepared.[16] A formal planning organization did not come into being until December 1964, when the Ministry of Economic Development was created and immediately charged with the task of producing the first national development plan. Since then, development planning has become a major policymaking activity.

Up to the end of the third plan period (1974–1978), participation in development planning was a restricted affair. Even with the introduction of development committees in the mid-1960s and the district planning exercise in 1974–1975, the situation did not change. The intention to involve lower level units in planning had been expressed, but it was not meaningfully practiced. Decisions and policies that mattered continued to be formulated at ministry headquarters and were expressed in the sectoral plans.

The key actors in the planning process, beginning in 1964, were the senior professionals and their expatriate advisers and counterparts. An experiment with a cabinet development committee was short-lived,[17] and the idea of creating a planning advisory committee[18] in which the private sector would be represented was not even given a chance for implementation.

Toward the end of the third plan period (1974–1978), the idea to organize sectoral working groups was born. The fourth plan benefited directly from the work of these groups, as have all the plans prepared since then.

As indicated, the working groups are usually organized on a sectoral basis and are composed of civil servants, expatriate advisers, and some local academics. The main task of the members during the planning period is the preparation of background policy papers for group discussion. The papers are often prepared by individuals regarded as knowledgeable in relevant fields. The policy papers are usually prepared in consultation with headquarters as well as with field-level officials.

The general practice is to break up a sector (for example, agriculture) into its smaller components (food production, commodity pricing and marketing, farm inputs, and so on). Ideas generated and accepted are then integrated into a sectoral draft plan for discussion by senior government officials on an interministerial basis. It is the duty of the Ministry of National Planning to put the draft national plan together for approval by the appropriate political authorities before the final plan is printed.

The work of sectoral planners is coordinated by the respective planning units or divisions within the individual ministries. It is the duty of the planning units to identify the participants and to ensure their full involvement. The approach has improved interactions tremendously both within and between ministries during the planning process. Policy outputs are now more fully assured of having broad agreement within government.

Presidential Committees and Commissions

Since independence many African governments have made frequent use of committees or commissions set up by the head of government or state to probe into a particular policy problem. These problems have usually centered around human needs, deprivation, and dissatisfactions that are identified by a leader or by others, and for which relief is sought.[19]

In Kenya, policymaking through the institution of presidential commissions is now a well-established approach. Once appointed, a committee or commission receives general and specific powers. Depending on the nature of the problem, the coverage can be extensive or it can be confined to a specific organization or a geographic area.

The committees have always worked in the open by inviting and receiving written and oral submissions from both experts and the general public. Various committees have worked from six months to two years, depending on the magnitude of the problem being addressed.

In the end, a report is produced based on an analysis of the information received from individual and group submissions as well as from other relevant secondary sources. The report is then subjected to close study by the head of state and his aides to identify aspects of the recommendations that can be implemented. The recommendations are then drafted into a sessional paper by the appropriate authority and subsequently forwarded to Parliament for debate and approval. Some areas where committee reports have been used as sources of policy pronouncements include: the civil service, education and training, local government, manpower and employment, parastatals, and investment strategy.[20]

The committee/commission approach has been institutionalized in the public policy process of Kenya and has been one of the most effective ways of involving the general public in the policy process. This approach, however, has not been without its critics.

In a number of cases, commissions have been established to make recommendations about decisions that have already been made by the executive. The Mackay Committee on the establishment of a second university is a good example. By the time the committee was established, a decision had already been made by President Moi to establish the second university in his home district at Eldoret.[21] Among other things, the committee was charged with examining the feasibility of establishing such an institution, when it should more appropriately have focused on the modalities of establishing the institution. In other instances, a number of salary review commissions have been created after decisions were already made to increase salaries.

The creation of some committees or commissions have served as delaying actions on the part of the state. Indeed, it is possible to view the creation of some committees and commissions as a way of generating consensus around decisions previously made, or for the purpose of depersonalizing the context of decisionmaking once a pronouncement has been made by the executive. Notwithstanding the potential strength inherent in the committee/commission approach, the policy recommendations of these groups have more often than not reinforced the status quo and failed to benefit those who need state intervention the most through such policy instruments.

For example, the Ndegwa Commission on Unemployment (1991)[22] should have recommended policies to narrow the widening gap between the rich and the poor. Instead, the commission's recommendations most probably widened the gap even more by advocating such measures as freedom for civil servants to engage in business activities, and the introduction of a variety of fringe benefits for senior civil servants, such as free use of state vehicles and state-subsidized domestic servants.

Explanations for such behavior may be found in the selection process of committee/commission membership, which has tended to be confined to those with known present or past association with the regime. These were men and women who share similar values regardless of their institutional affiliations.

The Participatory Approach

Two policies have been associated with the participatory approach, namely, the 1981 National Food Policy and the policies under the District Focus for Rural Development Strategy, introduced in 1983.[23]

As a policymaking strategy, the participatory approach involves the holding of a structured seminar on a particular policy. Initially, the key organization or organizations concerned with implementation are asked to prepare papers stating the nature of the policy in detail as well as their perceived role in the implementation of the policy. These ideas, together with other seminar contributions, are then synthesized into a policy document. The latter subsequently forms the basis of future seminars, undergoing revisions until a final version is produced.

The success of the approach is premised on the interaction between policymakers (both political and administrative) and the policy implementors. The seminars are arranged both at the center and at various administrative units in the field. At some point the seminars become awareness oriented, as the characteristics of the policy are explained to late-entry participants (usually lower-level actors). The seminars appear to be an ideal approach in formulating policies whose successful implementation depends on wide, popular support.

The Case of National Food Policy

The background to this policy was the food crisis of 1980, occasioned largely by maladministration. It began with a bumper maize harvest in 1976–1977; the Cereals and Produce Board filled its stores to capacity with purchases from farmers. In 1977–1978, the board was unable to reach its usual level of purchasing. As a result, many farmers with poor or no on-farm storage facilities suffered great losses. This situation discouraged them from planting during the next season. Meanwhile, the board had decided to reduce its stock through export sales. By mistake, the national strategic reserves were tapped. By the time the mistake was realized it was too late. The 1978–1979 harvest was meager, and the board could not satisfy public demand during 1979–1980. By 1980, the problem had reached crisis proportions with long food queues forming all over the country. The government was forced to import yellow maize from the United States. It was against this background that the 1981 National Food Policy was formulated.

The initiative came from the president, who wanted to avoid such a crisis in the future. The then chief secretary established a framework for the preparation of a food policy. The setting was the Ministry of Agriculture (the Planning Division), where background papers were commissioned on various aspects of the policy. The preparation of the policy was a joint effort between Kenyan bureaucrats and various technical assistance groups. The Harvard advisory group, then operating in the Ministry of Agriculture, had significant input as did other expatriate advisers attached to the Office of the President (Policy Analysis Unit).

Seminars were held to discuss the papers at the Kenya Institute of Administration, near Nairobi, and later in the provinces and districts. The purpose of the seminars was to involve both local-level staff and members of the farming community responsible for implementation.

The policy was expected to remain in force until 1989 and to center on food production. It was an effective weapon in the hands of the bureaucrats to convince the political leadership that, at long last, a well-thought-out food policy was in place.

There was significant commitment to the policy from 1981 to 1984.[24] In 1984, the country experienced a massive drought and some food had to be imported. This condition presented an opportunity to the proponents of balanced crop development (that is, food and cash crops) to intervene to change the policy. The need for expanding acreage for export cash crops was stressed and finally found expression in the 1986 *Sessional Paper* on economic management.[25]

The supporters of cash crop expansion argued that it was the surest way to mobilize the foreign exchange needed to import food when droughts or unexpected food crises occurred. Other policy areas such as marketing and farm subsidies were also revised in response to structural adjustment interventions.

By 1986, the 1981 food policy had been virtually abandoned, three years earlier than expected. The experience showed both the strengths and the weaknesses of the policy process. The food policy's most important success was the use of seminars that involved local-level staff and farmers as well as administrators and politicians in policy development and implementation issues. The high level of commitment given to the policy during the period 1981–1984 illustrates the merits of employing an open participatory approach.

With the drought and subsequent food imports in 1984, the policy was increasingly coopted by consultants financed by USAID and, in particular, the Harvard Institute of International Development, which was working in the Ministry of Agriculture. Critics have argued that these individuals lacked both the technical knowledge and a sensitivity to the local situation. Although the policy began with significant potential for institutional development, its success was undercut during a period of crisis by the intervention of technical assistance groups.

The District Focus Strategy

The District Focus for Rural Development can be described as a procedural policy, one dealing with how government is organized and how it conducts its business.[26] Decentralization is a good example of a procedural policy, and it is what the district focus strategy is all about. The success of a procedural policy requires the involvement of those whose work procedures are affected by the policy. Accordingly, the architects of the policy opted for the open participatory approach.

As conceived, the policy was intended to address the problem of concentrated decisionmaking powers at ministry headquarters, thus improving management efficiency in the development process.[27] The roots of the policy can be found in a 1971 civil service review commission report and, more recently, in a 1982 report on government expenditure.[28]

The district focus recommendations were accepted, and the president announced the decision to adopt the policy in September 1982. Up to this point, no other institution had been involved. Once the decision had been taken, however, the next step was to ensure the widest possible involvement in its elaboration and in the preparation of the implementation strategy. This step was meant to gain the acceptance of those whose support was considered crucial to the policy's success.

Seminars were organized at the Kenya Institute of Administration for senior civil servants and national-level politicians to discuss both the idea in general terms and ways in which the policy could be fleshed out. Seminars were also held in the provinces and districts to involve those in the field, on whom the success of the policy hinged.

By 1983, a policy document was produced outlining the characteristics of the policy. The document was later revised through more seminars and workshops.[29] In the meantime, central coordinating committees were created and the number of awareness seminars increased.

Studies of the district focus policy suggest that of all the decentralization policies the government has tried since independence, this has been the most successful.[30] Because of the policy, the financial management of district-specific projects now occurs at the district level, more senior personnel are operating at the district level, and development committees have significant input at the project identification stage.

The success of the policy can be attributed to the commitment of top political leadership. Such an open commitment has been responsible for the policy's acceptance by even those ministries that in the past have shown reluctance to implement any form of decentralization policy. The effective mobilization of the people involved in the implementation of the policy was another important factor contributing to its success. Moreover, there was very little, if any, involvement by non-Kenyans in the formulation of this policy. The ideas that found their way into the policy were generated at the seminars organized and directed by Kenyans.

A number of lessons can be learned from the district focus case. The design and structure within which the policy was formulated appear to have facilitated its success. The policy was developed for and with the involvement of the people affected by the policy. An ongoing and visible commitment by Kenya's political leadership persuaded reluctant ministries to stay with the policy. Finally, there was marginal input from external actors. The policy's success owes much to Kenyan ownership of the policy process in this instance. Gaining the acceptance of all the relevant actors at various stages of the process kept up the momentum and ensured the widest possible involvement of those whose support was necessary for policy sustainability.

Achievements and Limitations

Generally speaking and in comparison with other African administrations, the Kenyan bureaucracy has done reasonably well in the management of national development. A review of national development plans produced since independence reveals that there has been progress on many fronts, which can be attributed to the efforts of the civil service. Kenya has also recorded satisfactory achievements in many sectors of the economy. As would be expected of any developing country, there have also been many frustrations, suggesting that more could have been done.

In the 1970–1974 plan, implementation problems from the first plan period were cited. These problems included a lack of commitment to plan policies and programs, inadequate project preparation, insufficient coordination, scarcity of key personnel, and inadequate organization of rural development strategies.[31] Over the years, subsequent plans have enumerated other problems such as the fragmented and ad hoc nature of policymaking, lack of initiative, poor organizational climate, lack of trained policy analysts, poor deployment practices, and lack of operational support.

These problems have adversely affected the implementation of development policies. Indeed, an authoritative government report has pointed out that "many policies agreed by Cabinet have been unnecessarily delayed or distorted during the implementation."[32] The report goes on to observe that midway through the 1979–1983 plan period, for example, little work had been done to implement about half of the cabinet decisions recorded in the policy chapter of the plan, and added that "the poor implementation of hard policy choices has contributed significantly to the present [that is, 1982] financial crisis and at the same time has reduced government impact on development."[33]

To improve the policy process, the working group issuing the report advocated a process that stressed policy and program analysis.[34] The working group also lamented that, despite active government support, the staff training program for the civil service had not been carefully planned and coordinated.[35] The report concluded that improving management was the most pressing issue government faced.[36] In the current plan (1989–1993), the government again observed: "Currently there is no effective monitoring and evaluation system that can provide information necessary to indicate the extent to which the process of development programming meets set objectives."[37]

In proposing a solution, the plan advocated that a secretariat be established, building on the monitoring and evaluation unit already existing in the Ministry of Planning and National Development.[38] However, the unit referred to is underdeveloped and needs to be expanded and strengthened. Reference was also made to the planned establishment of supportive sectoral policy committees to facilitate integrated evaluation of emerging issues.[39]

The question that needs to be addressed at this point is: What is the source of this policy management problem? A partial explanation lies in Kenya's colonial heritage. During the colonial period, the structure of administration was highly compartmentalized within the hierarchy of authority, which extended from headquarters in Nairobi down to the provinces and districts. A similar situation occurred within departments, by division, location, and sublocation. A culture of "departmentalism" and the relative autonomy that goes with it was inherited intact, in spite of the *majimbo* (regional) constitution.

During the first plan period (revised 1966–1970), a need for some integration through a network of development committees was recommended, both at the center and in the field. Department-level staff were unenthusiastic. Attendance at committee meetings at the district level was irregular, and committees were not seriously regarded.[40] Over the years, however, and especially since the introduction of the district focus strategy, there have been some noticeable, positive changes, but much remains to be done.

What "departmentalism" means in the context of policy development is that each ministry enjoys a good deal of autonomy over its own policies relative to other ministries. The result is a lack of cooperation and coordination, even where such joint activity is a condition for success.

The relationship that a ministry head cultivates with key staff is another critical variable in policy management. It has been alleged that lack of consultation is common. So is lack of effective delegation. Both of these create an unhealthy organizational climate, making group decisionmaking almost impossible. Good policies require substantive input from all those concerned. There are few ministries that follow a collective decisionmaking system outside of the development planning framework discussed above.

In practical terms, only the Ministry of National Planning and Development has established a special unit for policy development. However, it has yet to be appropriately staffed and utilized. Most of the large ministries still rely on ad hoc working groups and donor-supported policy interventions. The policymaking process continues to be characterized by lack of functional integration among the ministries and between the center and the field agencies.

The tendency in the case of center-field relationships is to regard the field merely as a source of data. But it is common knowledge that their data base is quite weak. As a result, policies are made that have only a marginal bearing on reality.

A major missing link in policy management in Kenya is the lack of an institutionalized process of policy analysis that would assist in the "systematic investigation of alternative policy options and the assembly and integration of evidence for and against each option."[41] Such a process would enable the development manager to assess a policy in terms of costs and benefits, both direct and indirect, and to examine implementation constraints and opportunities. The process is lacking in Kenya, precisely because of the ad hoc nature of policymaking.

The situation in the elected, local authorities is even worse than that in the central government. Local authorities have a weak resource base and a poorly trained staff. A weak resource base has forced them to rely on the central government for survival. As a result, they have lost the relative autonomy promised in their charters of incorporation. Over the years, they have operated as mere field agencies of the central government. The center's weak capacity for policy analysis has had a direct effect on them as well.

However, the context of policymaking by the local authorities has changed since the introduction of the district focus strategy.[42] Policymaking activities now center around the District Development Committee (DDC), rather than the Ministry of Local Government. Dependence on the central government remains significant, however, as the DDCs lack capacity to formulate policies on their own.[43] Building capacity at this level remains a development management priority if decentralization efforts are to be successful.

Improving the Policy Management System

This chapter has demonstrated that there is a need to improve the policy management system within the bureaucracy through strengthening existing organizations and/or creating new ones. One way of upgrading the quality of policymaking in Kenya would be to improve the analytical skills of the staff involved in policymaking. The various aspects of project management also need more attention, especially problem identification and definition, the preparation of feasibility studies, and monitoring and evaluation techniques.

Currently, policy coordination rests with the cabinet office. However, as a United Nations report observed, the office is not adequately staffed to discharge that responsibility effectively.[44] To continue playing that role, the office needs to expand both its staff and scope of activities. An expanded office could be responsible for policy initiation, development, coordination, monitoring, and evaluation. Similar units could also be created within individual ministries and in the field with a framework established that would link the ministry organizations to the cabinet office on a routine basis (studies and seminars). The United Nations' Special Action Programme in Administration and Management (SAPAM) activities could be expanded to pursue these institution-building efforts.[45] Alternatively, there exists the possibility of forming a national center for policy studies, similar to India's Centre for Policy Research or Nigeria's National Institute of Policy and Strategic Studies.[46]

A high-quality program for policy management must also pay attention to human resource development. Kenya has a reservoir of well-educated staff that could be trained as policy analysts at minimal cost. For example, the Kenya Institute of Administration could be strengthened to support such a training program.[47] Another consideration is the development of a postgraduate program in public administration at the University of Nairobi, with a special focus on policy analysis.

Conclusion

Of the three sociopolitical influences on policy formulation in Kenya, the nature of the economy and the bureaucracy appear to be the major ones. The openness of the economy has encouraged greater external intervention in the policy process. The executive, through its administrative arm, has emerged as the dominant policy actor. This conclusion is supported by the key roles the executive and the donor agencies play in the initiation and determination of Kenya's policy agenda.

The country's track record in policy implementation is satisfactory, but institutional bottlenecks continue, and they have inhibited the smooth management of the policy system. The missing links appear to be the lack of well-developed policy analysis units, weak policy-related skills in the various government ministries, and the absence of input from organizations outside of government. As a result, policy analysis, evaluation, and feedback—all so critical to the success of development efforts—are weak or nonexistent.

Notes

1. Raymond A. Bauer and Kenneth J. Gergen, eds., *The Study of Policy Formulation* (New York: The Free Press, 1968), p. 3.

2. J. F. Anderson, *Public Policy-Making* (New York: Praeger Publishers, 1975), p. 29.

3. Colin Leys, *Underdevelopment in Kenya: The Politics of Neo-Colonialism* (Berkeley: University of California Press, 1975).

4. David K. Leonard, *African Successes: Four Public Managers of Kenyan Rural Development* (Berkeley: University of California Press, 1991).

5. Walter O. Oyugi, "Uneasy Alliance: Party-State Relations in Kenya," in *Politics and Administration in East Africa*, ed. Walter O. Oyugi (Nairobi: Konrad Adenauer Foundation, 1992).

6. Ibid.

7. Republic of Kenya, *National Development Plan 1989–1993* (Nairobi: Government Printer, 1989), p. 63.

8. Ibid., p. 71.

9. Walter O. Oyugi, "Role of Technical Assistance in National Development: The Case of Kenya," in *Technical Assistance Administration in East Africa*, ed. Y. Tandon (Stockholm: Almquist and Wiksell, 1973); Gerald Holtham and Arthur Hazlewood, *Aid and Inequality in Kenya: British Development Assistance to Kenya* (London: Croom-Helm, 1976); and Walter O. Oyugi, *Rural Development Administration: A Kenyan Experience* (New Delhi: Vikas Publishing Co., 1981).

10. Republic of Kenya, *Report of Commission of Inquiry, Public Service Structure and Remuneration Committee* (Nairobi: Government Printer, 1971).

11. Republic of Kenya, *Sessional Paper No. 10 on African Socialism and Its Application in Planning to Kenya* (Nairobi: Government Printer, 1965).

12. Cherry Gertzel, *The Politics of Independent Kenya* (Evanston, Ill.: Northwestern University Press, 1970).

13. Republic of Kenya, *Sessional Paper No. 1 on Economic Management* (Nairobi: Government Printer, 1986).

14. *Accelerated Development in Sub–Saharan Africa* (Washington, D.C.: World Bank, 1981).

15. Leonard, *Management Successes*, p. 222.

16. D. Ghai, "The Machinery of Planning in Kenya" (Brighton: Institute of Development Studies, Sussex Conference Paper, 1969).

17. Ibid.

18. Republic of Kenya, *National Development Plan 1970–1974* (Nairobi: Government Printer, 1970).

19. For example, see J. F. Anderson, *Public Policy-Making*, p. 55.

20. For example, see the following Rebublic of Kenya reports: *Report of Commission of Inquiry* (see Note 10, above); *Report of the Civil Service Review Committee 1979–1980* (1980); *Kenya Education Commission Report* (1964); *Working Paper on the Second University* (1981); *Presidential Working Party on Education and Training for the Next Decade and Beyond* (1981); *Report of the Presidential Commission on Unemployment* (1983); *Report of the Presidential Commission on Unemployment* (1991); *Review of Statutory Boards* (n.d.); and *Working Paper on Government Expenditures* (1982). (All published in Nairobi by the Government Printer.)

21. Republic of Kenya, *Working Paper on the Second University.*

22. Republic of Kenya, *Report on Unemployment.*

23. Republic of Kenya, *Sessional Paper No. 4 on National Food Policy* (Nairobi: Government Printer, 1981); and Republic of Kenya, *District Focus for Rural Development Strategy*, revised (Nairobi: Government Printer, 1987).

24. Walter O. Oyugi, "Kenya: The Implementation of the 1981 National Food Policy" (unpublished paper, 1992).

25. Republic of Kenya, *Sessional Paper No. 1.*

26. J. F. Anderson, *Public Policy-Making*, p. 55.

27. For example, see Republic of Kenya, *District Focus.*

28. Republic of Kenya, *Report of Commission of Inquiry;* Republic of Kenya, *Working Paper on Government Expenditures.*

29. Republic of Kenya, *District.*

30. Walter O. Oyugi, "Kenya: Two Decades of Decentralization Efforts," *African Administrative Studies*, no. 26 (1986), pp. 133–161; Walter O. Oyugi, "Decentralization Development Planning and Management in Kenya: An Assessment," in *Decentralization Policies and Socio-Economic Development in Sub-Sahara Africa*, ed. Ladipo Adamolekun et al. (Washington, D.C.: World Bank, 1990).

31. Republic of Kenya, *National Development Plan 1970–1974*, p. 71.

32. Republic of Kenya, *Working Paper on Government Expenditures*, p. 15.

33. Ibid.

34. Ibid., p. 70.

35. Ibid., p. 73.

36. Ibid., p. 74. See also United Nations, Development Administration Division, *Report of the Special Action Programme in Administration and Management: Programming Mission to Kenya (Nairobi, February 13 to March 16, 1989)* (New York: United Nations Development Programme, 1989), which reached similar conclusions about the management situation in Kenya. In particular, the report cited underdeveloped policy coordination methods, compartmentalism of policy issues, absence of periodic evaluation of policies, and lack of integration of resource inputs.

37. Republic of Kenya, *National Development Plan 1989–1993*, p. 40.

38. Ibid., p. 41.

39. Ibid.

40. Oyugi, "Kenya."

41. Jacob B. Ukeles, "Policy Analysis: Myth or Reality," *Public Administration Review*, vol. 37, no. 3 (May–June 1977), pp. 223–228.

42. Republic of Kenya, *District Focus.*

43. Oyugi, "Decentralization Development Planning."

44. United Nations, Development Administration Division, *Report of the*

Special Action Programme.

45. In order for the SAPAM program to succeed in this regard, four things would have to happen: (1) the program would have to sell itself better than it has done so far; (2) the program would have to move from its present low-profile status to one in which it becomes a major catalyst in policy initiative. To achieve this goal, the program would have to find ways and means of assisting key ministries such as industry, agriculture, treasury, and education to establish policy analysis units of their own, and thereafter assist them in establishing their own mechanisms of operation; (3) the program would have to mobilize resources from many donor sources and, in doing so, impress upon the donors the need for cooperation versus competition, which is presently the case; and (4) the program would need to commission policy studies and hold interministerial seminars to establish a linkage framework.

46. V. Moharir, "Institutionalization of Policy Analysis in Developing Countries: An Explanatory Approach," in *Bureaucracy and Developmental Policies in the Third World*, ed. H. K. Asmerom, Robert Hoppe, and R. B. Jain (Amsterdam: Vu University Press, 1992). As Moharir noted, the two institutions are financed by their respective governments, which also appoint the leading staff, although they are independent with regard to selection of issues and publication of results. Drawing upon the experiences of these institutions, there appears to be no reason why the Kenyan government could not create such an institution and initiate policy studies that it could then have the right to have published under confidential or restricted circulation. The key question, however, is whether the establishment of such an institution is a guarantee for improving the quality of public policy management.

47. In fact, the current GOK/UNDP policy support project (SAPAM), based at the Kenya Institute of Administration, could form the basis for the establishment of such a center. Once established, authorities in the field of policy analysis, both local and expatriate, could be identified and invited from time to time to conduct relevant courses.

7

Botswana: Confronting the Realities of Capacity Building

Keshav C. Sharma & Elvidge G. M. Mhlauli

Starting from Scratch

Many countries on the African continent are characterized by economic crisis, political instability, and regional-ethnic tensions. Critics have also regularly taken note of the tendency of African countries to mismanage resources and of their poor human rights records, lack of integrity in the civil service, and authoritarian political leadership. Botswana, by contrast, has experienced political stability and sustained economic growth and has been relatively free of regional and ethnic tensions. A World Bank study appropriately concluded that Botswana "has built an enviable reputation as having one of the most effective public sector managements in Africa, and indeed among developing countries."[1] It is worthwhile to more closely examine Botswana's achievements in light of the present attention being given to the need for rapid and effective political and economic reform.

Botswana has been pointed to as a model of success,[2] but its early beginnings were not hopeful. When the nation became independent in 1966 its GDP per capita was one of the lowest in the world, and the country was grouped among the least developed. During the protectorate period, Britain showed little interest in the territory because it was convinced that the country had no natural resources of consequence and was not attractive to capital investment. As a result of such thinking, Botswana experienced eighty years of colonial neglect.

With independence the government set off on a course of economic and social development, creating an infrastructure that included a new capital, roads, electricity, schools, hospitals, a civil service, a police force, and, some years later, a defense force. A number of development plans were formulated and implemented for economic development and social welfare. The stated objectives of Botswana's development policy are rapid economic growth, economic independence, sustained development, and social justice.

Considerable achievements have been made in terms of economic growth as Botswana has moved from a traditional economy based on cattle raising to a dualistic economy led by a small but vigorous modern sector.[3] Shifts in the pattern of domestic production and in the sources and levels of income since independence have been dramatic, although domestic production is strongly dominated by minerals and the economy heavily depends on trade. Moreover, the capital-intensive nature of mineral production and of the modern sector generally has not provided as much new employment as was originally anticipated.

At independence Botswana depended on substantial grants to cover its budget deficit, had no financial reserves, and had an infrastructure totally inadequate for any significant economic growth. Faced with such challenges, the government adopted the politics of development over the politics of ideology.[4] This has resulted in the careful husbanding of revenue, the limitation of expenditure to essentials, and a deliberate, concentrated effort to finance only those projects essential to economic growth. As a result, Botswana's public debt has been managed responsibly and most of the trappings of power have been shunned.[5]

The Pursuit of Realistic Development Strategies

The government's overall economic strategy has been to achieve rapid and large returns from intensive capital investment in mining, particularly the country's large diamond reserves, and to reinvest those returns to improve the living standards of those who do not benefit directly from mining sector expansion. Further, government policies have emphasized the complementary themes of employment creation and rural development, including improvements in infrastructure, education, and health facilities. The highest proportion of government investment to date (including the investment program of parastatals) has gone to build up the basic infrastructure of the country. Despite its efforts, the country has been less than successful in diversifying its economy and expanding economic growth to the rural areas, where more than 80 percent of the Batswana live.

Government development plans are not intended to stifle private initiative but rather to create favorable conditions in which the private sector can contribute to Botswana's development.[6] In fact, more than 80 percent of Botswana's GDP is produced by the private sector. The private sector also actively participates in the planning process through such advisory committees as the National Employment, Manpower and Incomes Advisory Board (NEMIC), and the National Technical Training Advisory Committee.

As in Kenya and Nigeria, there has been a strong orientation toward market-oriented policies and private investment. Both foreign and domestic private investment have been welcomed. Botswana's National Development Plan 6 recognizes the benefits of a market-oriented system for Botswana, noting that the system is more efficient in producing goods and services, and is more economical in the use of scarce administrative capacity. The plan also stresses that the principal means for initiation and ownership of industry and trade is the private sector and that there will be a continuing need for foreign investment, especially in those areas where the necessary skills and technologies are not available locally.

Like the other market-oriented African states (Kenya, Nigeria, and the Côte d'Ivoire), the Botswana economy has not escaped the economic downturn of the late 1980s. Unlike the experience of these other countries, however, the country's frugal fiscal policies have allowed it to avoid extensive external debt and the need for stabilization and structural adjustment programs.

Botswana has also escaped an important budget constraint so familiar in other African countries. Public enterprises in Botswana are fairly efficient and do not strain the national budget. Botswana is also one of the few countries in Africa that has a convertible currency. Given the potential for success, Botswana has attracted a sizable proportion of donor funding over the years. This technical assistance generally has been utilized prudently, and Botswana's credibility with donor agencies has consistently remained high.

Botswana's Developmental State

The relationship between political leadership and the bureaucracy has undergone significant changes in many African countries since independence. The emergence of military rule and one-party states has resulted in relationships quite different from those of the British model, which emphasizes the neutrality of the civil service. The cumulative effect of such changes has been to move many African countries away from the ideals of the development-oriented state that so predominated early postindependence thinking. By contrast,

Botswana has been able to retain a functioning multiparty system with free and fair elections.

Racial, religious, ethnic, or regional tensions have been negligible. Corruption in political leadership and in public service circles has been limited, although in the last five years, the country has gone through a number of corruption scandals that have decreased the credibility of what historically has been an efficient and effective state administration. To be sure, the issue of corruption has been addressed quickly and openly. Implicated political leaders, including the former vice-president, Peter Mmusi, promptly lost their jobs. President Ketumile Masire has advised those who seek to compromise the principle of integrity and who exhibit partisan inclinations to resign from public service and practice their politics in the open with a clear conscience.[7]

Pursuing the politics of development in Botswana has produced a political elite who have assumed the role of modernizers. This role has placed emphasis on and responsibility for developing the country to the highest possible level given its economic resources. Botswana has gone far to meet the challenge of establishing a development-oriented administration. Such a commitment to development management is unusual in Africa.[8]

Rather than rapidly localize its public service at independence, the leadership has pursued a policy of gradual localization and, as has been the case in Kenya, made liberal use of expatriate advisers, technicians, and administrators who over the years were given substantive authority with little political interference. On the whole, the country's experience with expatriate personnel has been congenial and productive, although the government periodically comes under mild attack for not moving more quickly on localization.

Since independence, the government has taken responsibility for educating the labor force that is required by the economy and is itself the largest single employer. Overall, the government defines the legal, fiscal, and monetary framework within which all sectors of the economy operate and has the responsibility for securing favorable international economic arrangements for domestic producers and consumers.

*The Machinery for Public Policymaking
and Development Planning*

A cabinet led by the president and a parliament including the representatives of opposition parties compose Botswana's highest authority for public policymaking and development planning. Below this level, the Ministry of Finance and Development Planning plays a central role. There is also active participation by the Directorate of Public Service Management, the Department of Statistics, the Bank of Botswana, and the planning units of various ministries and district-level organizations.

A joint ministry that combines finance and development planning and is responsible for planning and budgeting has been quite successful in Botswana. This institutional arrangement has helped to promote coordination between planning and budgeting activities and has avoided the many planning and budgeting conflicts that are common in other developing countries. Another important feature of the development planning process has been the posting to various ministries of planning officers belonging to a common cadre controlled by the Ministry of Finance and Development Planning.

The most significant organization for major policy decisions and development strategy is the economic committee of the cabinet, which consists of all the ministers and permanent secretaries, the head of the police, the commander of the defense force, and the governor of the Bank of Botswana.

Decentralization in Development Planning

Decentralized planning and district-level planning structures are also characteristic of the Botswana policy process. According to the District Planning Handbook of the Government of Botswana:

> The overriding aim of the District Planning process is to provide a decentralized planning and implementation capacity which is sensitive and responsive to needs, problems and priorities of local communities. . . . It must recognise the need for a high level of local participation if development activities are to have an impact and to be sustained over the long run. The concept is one of "bottom-up" planning and development that will have critical inputs into the formation of national policies and programmes.[9]

Decentralized, district-level, development-planning exercises have faced a number of problems, however, which need to be addressed in order to bridge the gap between the intention and the reality of a decentralized process. These problems include policy formulation, implementation, monitoring, and guidance as well as difficulties in establishing both vertical and horizontal communication flows.

The nature of the planning process in Botswana has been described as "top-down" planning, as opposed to "bottom-up" planning.[10] Development plans are formulated at the national level.

Although the contribution of district-level organizations has been steadily increasing, their impact on the policy process remains limited. More often than not, consultations between the national and district level take the form of an explanation of policies or elaboration of plans formulated at the higher levels of government.

Ministry field staff in the districts either receive communication about the contents of their district plan through instructions from the ministry, or they wait until they hear from their headquarters before presenting their submissions to the district plan managers. In some cases, office equipment and computers for district-level staff is marginal. This is particularly true in the field offices of ministries. As a result, district-level staff are often unable to make any worthwhile contribution to the planning exercise and depend on assistance from above.

In general, communication links between the center and the districts are ineffective, with district-level staff lacking adequate, satisfactory, and timely information. This inefficiency is due in part to large staff turnover at headquarters or to the posting of relatively junior staff in such positions. It is also partly due to insufficient sensitivity on the part of some officers in providing prompt and adequate responses.

It is fair to conclude that district-level planning deserves to be taken more seriously by the central planners. District-level planning structures and processes need to be further strengthened before decentralization efforts are fully realized. Planning has to be done not only in terms of the professional caliber and training of relevant staff, but also in terms of staff commitment to the task at hand.

Administrative Capacity and Local Authorities

With a view to promoting decentralization, Botswana has created district councils, which are legal entities (statutory bodies) and instruments of political decentralization. They have been given responsibilities mainly for the administration of primary education, primary health services, construction and maintenance of rural roads, water supply, community development, and social welfare. Although their administrative capacity for the performance of these functions has been gradually improving, their influence remains limited.

The councils receive substantial financial assistance from the central government. Council staff are provided through a specially organized Unified Local Government Service (ULGS), now known as Local Government Service Management (LGSM). The councils also receive a great deal of assistance and guidance from central government ministries, and the central government exercises various kinds of controls over the councils that limit their autonomy. Limited administrative capacity can be primarily attributed to the weaknesses in political leadership, staffing, financial standing, and relations with the central government.

Heavy reliance on the central government and a high degree of control from the center have produced district councils that are limited in both function and autonomy. Given such constraints, the potential future growth of the councils into responsible bodies of local government is seriously inhibited, and, indeed, may defeat the very rationale for which they were originally created. In order to correct the situation, it is necessary for the central government to begin reducing its control, gradually increasing council autonomy as administrative capacity expands. Capacity building efforts in this instance will require additional training for both staff and councillors.

Grassroots Participation

During the last few years, administrative accountability and public responsibility have increased in Botswana through greater public awareness and political education. The current challenge is to make the bureaucracy more responsive and to develop closer, two-way communication between the government and the people. Government needs to know more about the needs, problems, priorities, expectations, and capacities of the people; and the public needs a better understanding of public policies, development strategies, development plan priorities, and the limitations and expectations of government. Public participation in development planning and public policymaking needs to become more meaningful and real in the future.

Increasing people's participation through decentralization efforts from the national level to the district level is a shift in the right direction. However, the process of decentralization will have to be extended to the subdistricts and the villages. Although the districts have complained about the lack of seriousness given to district-level decentralization, the districts themselves are not immune from such criticism. They have done very little to promote increased autonomy within subdistrict organizations or bodies such as village development committees or traditional institutions such as the *Kgotla* (village assembly). Decentralization is only partially complete if it stops at the district level. Village-level organizations will have to receive greater attention and autonomy if decentralization is to be fully carried out.

The Role of Public Enterprises in Development

Botswana's public enterprises, although limited in number, play a significant role in the country's economy.[11] Unlike parastatals in some other African countries, they have not have been organized for ideological reasons. Primarily, their role is to facilitate the development and management of certain activities of vital significance to the economy and to manage public utilities. The government has made it clear that it does not believe in nationalization.

Several government aims have been cited with regard to parastatals in both National Development Plans 6 and 7: They should promote the creation of new economic opportunities; avoid competing with Batswana entrepreneurs; positively assist citizen entrepreneurs to start up or to acquire or participate in viable businesses; and, where possible, sell off suitable ventures to Batswana owner-managers.[12]

The government has also encouraged public-private partnerships in vital sectors such as mining. For example, South African multinational firms have a significant position in the investment and management of Botswana diamond mines. To achieve a more proper balance in the relationship, their agreement also includes a substantial role for the Botswana government in the management of the mines.

Mismanagement and corruption in the parastatal sector have been limited in nature in Botswana. Moreover, some public enterprises, such as the Botswana Meat Commission, have earned substantial profits and have contributed to economic development.

Some institutional and organizational development problems persist among public sector enterprises, however. These include: a general lack of clarity regarding operational objectives and performance criteria, the absence of established standards and procedures for board-management relations and employer-employee relations, lack of effective control mechanisms, and a shortage of adequately trained and skilled manpower.

Critical Shortages of Qualified Manpower

A shortage of qualified manpower has been Botswana's biggest constraint in increasing administrative capacity. At the time of independence the country had very few graduates, no university of its own, and a very small number of locals in senior positions of the public service. The magnitude of the shortage of qualified manpower is discernible from the fact that out of a very small establishment of 184 administrative posts in the public service at independence, only 24 positions were held by Batswana. Even at the lower levels, only 275 out of 613 positions in the technical, executive, and secretarial grades were held by local officers.[13]

The first government secondary school was started only in 1965. Up to 1964 there were only two mission schools and one school organized as a private venture. Moreover, in 1964 only twenty-seven students passed the Cambridge Overseas School Certificate. The independent University of Botswana was established in 1982. The latter replaced the University of Botswana and Swaziland (UBS), which was the direct successor to the University of Botswana, Lesotho and Swaziland (UBLS). In 1965, the UBLS had only twenty-three students from Botswana.

Since 1965, education in Botswana has expanded considerably. The number of secondary schools has grown steadily, vocational training institutions have been established, and training institutions like the Botswana Institute of Administration and Commerce and the Institute of Development Management have expanded greatly. The expansion of educational facilities is also evident in the physical development of the University of Botswana.

In spite of the rapid expansion, however, the development of managerial personnel in Botswana for both the public and private sectors has been constrained by inadequately developed educational facilities, the limited operations of training institutions, and problems with microlevel manpower planning.[14]

Although the senior positions of generalists in the public service have been localized (filled by Batswana) for some time, many professional positions continue to be held by expatriates (doctors, engineers, accountants, and so on), whose number has also increased in some cases due to expansion and development of public sector activities. The government of Botswana has adopted a realistic attitude toward localization and does not believe in localizing at the cost of efficiency. In some cases, for example, the government has also been prepared to delocalize certain positions (that is, secretaries for very senior officials in the public service, and for ministers) to maintain standards of efficiency and productivity.

Where localization has been accomplished, the government remains concerned about raising the standards of proficiency and productivity of personnel operating in the civil service, local authorities, parastatals, and private enterprises. In particular, administrative and managerial personnel need to be more sensitive and responsive to the aspirations and expectations of the population and to address the problems of productivity, discipline, morale, and incentives more adequately.

Conclusion

Botswana's prosperity and success can be attributed to a number of factors: the country's sound political leadership, pragmatic public policies, and prudent economic management. The country's mineral resources have also provided a steady source of revenue. In particular, Botswana's successes have been the result of its ability to bring together all these factors in a prudent and responsible manner.[15]

It has been observed that sustainable development requires a domestic capacity for the formulation and implementation of policy—a capacity that is rooted in the society, culture, and history of the country that it serves.[16] In economic policymaking Botswana's experience reveals that it has been prudent in organizing the roles of the public and private sectors, giving due consideration to the realities of domestic capacity.

Recognizing the limited capacity of the state, Botswana's political leadership chose not to overextend the public sector. The limited number of state-owned and controlled enterprises is a primary example of a pragmatic response to realistic capacity considerations. The slow pace with which localization has been pursued is another example. Where domestic experience, capital, and expertise have not been available, the government has not been reluctant to encourage foreign investment and multinational participation. Capacity considerations have also been evident in the government's willingness to encourage and experiment with various types of partnerships. For example, efforts in the mining sector have produced working partnerships between government and foreign investors. In the case of the Botswana Development Corporation (BDC), the government has been an active joint venture partner with indigenous entrepreneurs.

Capacity building considerations have also influenced the government's efforts to increase grassroots participation through strengthened local government organizations. Here the results are mixed. At both the district and subdistrict levels, the government has been repeatedly challenged to find innovative structures and processes that devolve authority and enhance participation. At issue has been the need to balance the demands for increased autonomy with the existing capacity to handle expanded responsibilities.

The democratic nature of Botswana civil society and its institutions and the economic policies under the leadership of Sir Seretse Khama and Sir Ketumile Masire have created an environment of peace and progress. The challenge has been to ensure that public policies do not result in the creation of wide disparities in wealth and income and that the benefits of growth do not accrue only to limited sections of the population. Should ownership and distribution issues become contentious, not only the prevailing peace and tranquility could be disturbed, but the very nature of Botswana's democratic institutions and the framework of present public policies could become questionable.

Focusing on pragmatism and productivity, Botswana has attempted to pursue more vigorously its efforts to build capacity in the civil service, parastatals, local government organizations, and private enterprise. It has remained steady in its commitment to achieving higher standards of integrity, efficiency, responsibility, and accountability.

Notes

1. Nimrod Raphaeli et al., *Public Sector Management in Botswana: Lessons in Pragmatism*, Staff Working Paper no. 709 (Washington, D.C.: World Bank, 1984).

2. Louis A. Picard, *The Politics of Development in Botswana: A Model for Success?* (Boulder, Colo.: Lynne Rienner Publishers, 1987).

3. As Lewis has observed, in all countries the economy and the society will show evidence of "dualism." Dualism is characterized by some sectors (mostly in agriculture but also in urban areas) that exhibit "low productivity, family-centered organization for business and farming, substantial overt and disguised unemployment, often considerable landlessness in the agricultural sectors, and relatively low income per capita." By contrast, the modern sectors will exhibit "larger organizations, wage employment at substantially higher skill and wage levels, more advanced technology, and correspondingly much higher income per capita." See Stephen R. Lewis, Jr., *The Economics of Apartheid* (New York: Council of Foreign Relations Press, 1990), p. 20.

4. Picard, *The Politics of Development.*

5. Raphaeli et al., *Public Sector Management.*

6. Government of Botswana, *National Development Plan 6: 1985–1991* (Gaborone: Government Printer, 1985).

7. The president, Sir Ketumile Masire, has expressed his unequivocal commitment to the principle of public service neutrality by pointing out that it is not possible for a civil servant who exudes partisan politics to be honest and dedicated in performing functions of public service. *Daily News* (Gaborone, Botswana), January 7, 1985.

8. Picard, *The Politics of Development.* The moderate stance of the ruling party, the Botswana Democratic Party (BDP), has also influenced the way the government has managed the economy. It has rejected both the extreme left and right, ethnic conservatism, and African socialism as all equally unacceptable development paths for Botswana.

9. Government of Botswana, Ministry of Local Government and Lands, *District Planning Handbook* (Gaborone: Government Printer, n.d.), pp. 6 and 79.

10. Picard, *The Politics of Development.*

11. Botswana's significant public enterprises cover manufacturing (Botswana Meat Commission), public utilities (Botswana Power Corporation and Botswana Water Utilities Corporation), livestock (Botswana Livestock Development Corporation), housing (Botswana Housing Corporation), banking (Bank of Botswana), promotional activities (National Development Bank), marketing (Botswana Agricultural Marketing Board), airways (Air Botswana), and general purpose economic development activity (Botswana Development Corporation).

12. Government of Botswana, *National Development Plan 6* and *National Development Plan 7: 1991–1997* (Gaborone: Government Printer, 1991).

13. C. Colclough and S. McCarthy, *The Political Economy of Botswana: A Study of Growth and Distribution* (London: Oxford University Press, 1980), p. 209.

14. J.C.N. Mentz and Louis A. Picard, "Localization in Botswana: A Reexamination" (Pittsburgh, unpublished paper, 1992).

15. Ibid.

16. See Louis A. Picard with V. Moharir and J. Corkery, "Capacity-Building for Policy Change and Sustainability: Lessons from the African Experience" (paper delivered to the Development Management Working Group, IIAS, Brussels, Belgium, October, 1990).

8

Sustainable Policies, Management Capacity, and Institutional Development

Louis A. Picard, Athumani J. Liviga
& Michele Garrity

The African participants at the June 1991 conference at Arusha, Tanzania, identified a number of critical issues relating to capacity building for policy change and sustainability. This chapter (based on the discussions at the conference) presents those issues within the broader context of four interlocking themes (see Chapter 1 and below) underlying policy reform efforts in Africa, and it attempts to capture the flavor of the dialogue at the meeting. Finally, the chapter posits ten summary statements that highlight the special problems and concerns characterizing structural adjustment programs in Africa.

The Appropriate Balance Between Public Sector and Private Sector Responsibilities

After independence, the state in many African countries was conceived of as a provider, intervening through state-owned and/or state-controlled enterprises or other means in virtually every area of economic and social life. In many cases the African state became a burden for development-related activity over time.

If the state is to accomplish its main objective—social and economic development—the role and scope of the state has to be restricted. Restricting state activity does not imply an abdication of responsibilities on the part of the state but, rather, a change in focus. In some instances, the state will be less involved while in others more state involvement will be needed. Moreover, each country has to develop the appropriate mix of public/private involvement that best represents the forces and influences most capable of effecting change within the national context.

Such public/private sector arrangements cannot be viewed as rigid in nature. Both the strengths and weaknesses of the public and private sectors have to be determined in assessing various policy alternatives, with the understanding that each partner must adapt to changing circumstances and that transitional phases could be necessary. To attempt to rationalize divisions of labor is probably not viable and all kinds of public-private partnerships should be explored. In the development of sustainable partnerships, it is essential to reconcile predictability and flexibility.

In managing economic and social development, the state should be responsible for the following three functions.

The state as provider. The state has responsibility for core activities such as the definition of a set of major policies for socioeconomic development; the provision of major infrastructure; and other activities related to national sovereignty issues such as national defense and foreign policy, financial policy, and the maintenance of public order.

The state as facilitator. The state has responsibility for the overall policies and the rules and regulations that create an enabling environment for economic growth and development, particularly for the indigenous African private sector. This also includes the development and promotion of the nongovernmental, not-for-profit sector.

The state in partnership. The state has responsibility for building a climate of cooperation and trust among the public, private, and not-for-profit sectors through efforts to develop more formal consultative mechanisms and for the transfer of ownership (both direct and indirect) of previously state-controlled and/or -managed activities.

There emerges in Africa a mixed picture of country-specific experiences in redefining and refocusing the role of the state with specific examples where grassroots organizations, the press, NGOs and PVOs (private voluntary organizations), interest-based groups, and the church have had some input into the policy process. Both the input and influence of nongovernmental actors have varied from one country to another due to degrees of openness, a lack of enthusiasm by key political actors to utilize societal-based institutions, lack of information and education, and low levels of understanding regarding specific policy implications and impacts.

In the African state there are difficulties in the implementation of policy. Both practitioners and academics in Africa recognize that in order to improve the quality of policies, increase the commitment of the implementation machinery, and enhance the sustainability of policies, there is a need to decentralize and increase participation at all levels of society. However, the nature of participation and, in particular, the multiparty political system remain controversial.

The processes and mechanisms of consultation, participation, and decentralization need to be refined and better understood by the key stakeholders in the policy process. Although consultation is a prerequisite for sustainability, the problem of continuous consultation needs to be avoided to prevent stalemate. Individuals as well as groups must trust their respective legal and political institutions to faithfully carry out the law. In the same vein, decentralization efforts should not become an attempt at microcontrol from the center.

Patterns of Decisionmaking:
The Nature of the State

There are two distinct components of decisionmaking: the decentralization of public sector decisionmaking to intermediate and primary units of government; and efforts to promote multiple channels of communication and influence between government and societal-based organizations.

Various countries have displayed differing degrees of centralization and decentralization in policymaking. The diversity of institutional frameworks and the presence of country-specific nomenclatures have also had a direct bearing on the nature of the policymaking process. More often that not, there is a gap between the form and the reality of institutional structures, with implications for both the mode of operation and effectiveness of decisionmaking. As a result, the actual process of policymaking is often quite different than the formal, institutional structures would indicate. The form versus reality issue is perhaps best exemplified by the dominance of the political executive in many countries.

In discussing the nature of the state and how it affects the policy process, a distinction needs to be made between differing types of government structures: the one-party state, the activist state with a civilian regime, and the activist state with a military regime. In the first two types of states, the basic, formal process through which policy proposals should go are present and honored, at least in the formal sense. Further, in a one-party state the speed of processing decisions is often related to the interest in the issue at hand by the head of state. Other major deficiencies of the one-party state include the absence of substantive opposition political activity; the relatively minor role that even the sole political party plays in the decisionmaking process; and, finally, the limitations on the articulation and aggregation of interests among all societal-based groups. By contrast, the civilian activist state allows many opportunities for extensive consultation between the government, donors, and interest groups, with the implications of implementation more likely to be examined.

In a military regime, the possibility of policy formulation by decree exists. Where policy is made by decree, more often than not there is a lack of analysis of problems, or of critical feasibility issues. As a result, downstream problems are likely to occur involving the availability of resources and/or interaction with other sectors. Under such circumstances, policy successes are often threatened from the beginning.

In all instances, however, the role of the state remains unclear, which posits the question of whether or not the role of the state can be articulated in a single statement that defines a regime type. In almost all African states, the strong, personalistic role of the African president limits debate and often results in impulsive, nonrational policymaking by fiat. For development to occur a strong predictable state is important because policy reform efforts require leadership by a diverse set of actors (both political and administrative) and the husbanding of scarce resources both inside and outside government.

Despite the problems inherent in defining specific state characteristics, any efforts to identify and determine the role of the state in the policy process must first address the nature of the state with respect to its decisionmaking structures, processes, and capacity. Issues of form versus reality are significant when it comes to making policy decisions stick, especially where the bureaucracy may resist policies. The tendency in some countries for bureaucracies to shelve, delay, or ignore policy directives has produced many policy failures, even where the political will to carry out reform has been high.

Much remains to be done to identify the necessary and appropriate organizational structures for building decisionmaking capacity. Attempts to decentralize government functions as well as efforts to promote pluralism in the broader societal context have been characterized by a rapid rise in new policy-oriented units and/or organizations. Although some African countries may need new organizational structures, consideration should be given to integrating new functions into existing structures for efficiency reasons. The overcommitment of scarce resources to new institutional arrangements is a major concern, as is the need to streamline and consolidate existing functions and responsibilities of the state. Such assessments should be directed at organizations operating outside of government as well.

In summary, the successful shift from a single center of decisionmaking to multiple channels of communication, discussion, and decisionmaking remains an open and unresolved question in many African countries. A number of the case studies described in this book show that even where multiple centers of decisionmaking occur, their influence can vary. Thus, many African states continue to be characterized by a lack of openness, a weak commitment to a transparent policy process, and little capacity to assess policy implications. In addition, the shift to multiple centers has been carried out with insufficient consideration for existing institutional capacity, and many of the evolving democracies in African remain fragile.

Solutions to issues of participation urgently require the development of an appropriate set of structures and processes that will clarify role definitions, develop organizations through strong education and training programs, assist in the creation of mechanisms of communication, and enhance the capacity for monitoring and evaluating policy decisions.

Building Implementation and Management Capacity

Policy management structures and processes in many African countries are weak and have been hindered by several factors. First, human resource development is critical; yet many aspects of human resource development have been overlooked or ignored in Africa. In particular, management skills are in short supply throughout the continent. Second, an important prerequisite for building policy implementation and management capacity is an understanding of the various threats and opportunities present in the political, economic, and social environment; yet stakeholder analysis is often absent from the policy process. Third, management issues must relate to both national and international circumstances and the role that donors play in the public management process; yet it is often the case that donor priorities prevail over domestic concerns. Fourth, more effort needs to be directed at bridging the gap between and among different sectors of the economy through the policy analysis process. Sectoral working groups have now become the norm in many African countries with regard to national planning exercises, but they have not been duplicated in other areas of government activity such as policy analysis.

Developing a strong capacity for policy analysis is directly related to the manpower available, to appropriate structures and management systems, and to the participation of a diverse set of actors. In the end, human resource development strategies provide the foundation for building implementation and management capacity. There are no shortcuts to ongoing institutional development, which is essential for political stability and economic development.

Finally, whether the intent is to create new structures and processes or to strengthen existing institutions, there is a need to clearly identify what is not working in order to begin the capacity building process. Institutional development activities should begin with the objective of giving governments an information base, analytical tools, and decision points. All are part of the sustainability process.

There are four prerequisites to strengthening the implementation and management capacity of national, subnational, functional, and sectoral organizations:

1. The specific roles of different organizations and actors relevant to the policy process should be clearly identified.
2. Where appropriate, such organizations should be endowed with adequate resources and training in the formulation and implementation of public policy.
3. Effective mechanisms should be developed to improve communication among the different actors and to facilitate the coordination of their activities.
4. Appropriate monitoring and evaluation mechanisms should be developed to ensure that problems are identified in a timely manner and that the appropriate remedial action is taken.

In varying degrees in many African countries the necessary analytical capacities for policy analysis are available; but these capacities are often misused due to misplacement and the misuse of personnel, the lack of essential tools, and lack of communication. Efforts needs to be made to bridge the gap between the supply and demand for these capacities. Both the scarcity of qualified personnel and the misplacement of personnel have contributed to the complexities and subtleties of policy implications being ignored.

The analytical capacities of policy units should have the following three components.

Quantitative techniques. These techniques are necessary for carrying out cost-benefit analysis as well as the overall and specific financial implications of various policy alternatives. They are also necessary for the appraisal of impacts, needs, and available resources.

Qualitative analysis. This component is necessary to assess feasibility, expectations, attitudes, and values. Such assessments identify the main actors in a given situation, establishing the potential winners and losers, and indicate the appropriate strategies for building consensus and coalitions between and among groups and individuals.

The legal framework. This component of policy analysis is often neglected but is necessary for both understanding the legal context in which policy alternatives will operate and the need to establish and/or amend relevant rules and regulations. Avoidance of rigid preconceptions of the private and public sector are also important in defining and implementing structural adjustment programs, as is the need for examining the merits of transitional phases during the implementation process.

Institutional Development and Sustainability

Institutional development and capacity building need to be considered within the larger context of developing sustainable policies. The implications and diverse issues of the present structural adjustment–induced environment are controversial, as are the dynamics and potential of the post–structural adjustment era. One point is clear, however: there is an overwhelming need to more effectively balance policy content considerations with institutional development and implementation considerations. The international donor community as well as African governments have been slow to recognize the capacity building demands of structural adjustment programs and their implications for sustainability.

Considering the poor state of economies in Africa, the policies advocated under structural adjustment seem to be unavoidable. To ensure sustainability, however, these policies must be indigenous and not donor imposed. Without exception, the prevailing country-specific conditions most often determine whether or not a structural adjustment package will be successful. Moreover, during the implementation phase of structural adjustment programs, there is a need to appreciate the limitations of criteria of efficiency and rationality advocated in the programs.

Policy management capacity has remained weak in Africa over the past thirty years, despite significant investment in human resource development. In part, this weakness is due to a lack of total institutional development, that is, the development of structures, processes, personnel, and systems appropriate to the specific political, economic, cultural, and social environment in which the policy process operates. Specifically, the following six issues should be addressed to ensure sustainability.

The institutional implications of specific policies. The manner and extent to which institutional implications are taken into account at the policy formulation stage has much to do with the sustainability of policies. The success or failure of different policies is closely related to the design of organizational structures and the processes of decisionmaking within institutions. Feasibility considerations, in particular, are important for the success and sustainability of policies. Resource allocations, manpower, acceptability, technical considerations, coordination, communication, and participation are all critical elements during the planning stage.

The enhancement of existing institutional resources. Enhancing the policy-oriented capacities of existing institutional resources is one promising avenue for ensuring sustainability. In general, these include universities, research institutions, and training organizations. Also important are government-related policy units, such as Nigeria's National Institute for Policy and Strategic Studies (NIPSS), and the Policy Analysis Unit in Kenya as well as similar units in NGO trade, business, agricultural, and labor organizations.

The improvement of information flows. Improving information flows throughout society can also enhance sustainability. Such efforts can assist in determining the needs and priorities of people at different levels of society and can raise the consciousness and awareness of the public of the capacities, role, and limitations of the state. Key organizations of civil society include the parliament, the media, interest-based groups, and public sector–oriented NGOs and community-based organizations. The development of different institutional and organizational arrangements for involving diverse groups in the process of consultation has begun to occur in a number of African countries as part of the democratization process. The effectiveness of these arrangements, however, has varied, and as a consequence, the sustainability of policies continues to be jeopardized.

In one-party states, for example, an elaborate structure exists in principle for linking the national level to the village level. In practice, however, this does not achieve participation. The Kenya experience with the seminar approach is an example of an attempt to energize the consultative-participative process. Nigeria also has a provision for public debate on issues of national importance. Such efforts are limited in practice, however, and many of the efforts are mechanical and informative rather than consultative. Underlying all of the approaches to the development of participative mechanisms are the issues of how to get people involved, who should participate at what levels in the policy hierarchy, and the need to distinguish between local and national policies.

The improvement of information systems. The creation and/or enhancement of policy-oriented information systems has not been adequately addressed in Africa. Analytical tools and the capacity to utilize various consultation/communication mechanisms are critical to institution building. The identification of decisionmaking points and systems that facilitate the capacity to clarify and, as necessary, review the roles of the several organizations and agencies involved in the policy process are essential to capacity building. Much needs to be done to develop management information systems that are appropriate to a resource poor environment.

The development of human resources. Although a few African countries still suffer from a lack of trained manpower, the problem in the majority of cases appears to be one of proper utilization of available manpower and the development of a suitable reward structure. The nature of the human resource shortage needs more careful analysis at both the national and local levels. It may be that an absolute shortage of requisite skills exists; in some cases, there may be a maldistribution of skills. While there may be talented people at the senior levels of the public service, there is often a severe shortage of skilled personnel at the middle level of the public sector. An important contributing factor that complicates the planning of strategies for human resource development is a lack of clarity in the role of the state in structural adjustment programs and policies. Inadequate personnel policies and systems have had a negative effect on the policy process and will continue to do so until the role of the state in development management and the nature of the skills shortage is more appropriately defined.

The twin issues of motivation and attitude are critical problems affecting human resource development. Structural adjustment programs have brought about a crisis with regard to compensation for public servants. Inadequate salaries have seriously affected the state's capacity to attract and retain staff persons of adequate caliber. In a broader context, attitudes shared by both civil servants and the general public regarding the value of public service have been seriously eroded, causing a crisis of morale. Moreover, structural adjustment programs have offered little to the general public or to the civil servant to replace the postindependence national feeling of good will felt toward national service that motivated so many in the early years of statehood.

There are several key areas where training needs to be strengthened. For example, human resource development efforts need to more closely focus on the importance of contextual factors in the policy process. These include national and international concerns and priorities as well as local and regional conditions. Policy planning, implementation, monitoring, and policy analysis activities all require a capacity to deal with elements of diverse environments that have an impact on internal management functions. Managers need to be able to distinguish between conditions that have to be taken as given and those problem areas that can be addressed. Constraints as well as opportunities must be recognized and incorporated into policy strategies. Personnel training in this regard is closely related to a host of governance issues that are both sensitive and complex but that need to be addressed.

The reordering of donor-client relations. Donors and host country program managers need to avoid the shortcomings that have resulted in poor policies in the past. It is important for recipient states to manage donors by requiring them to work within an institutional context. Although structural adjustment programs reduced waste and led to better policy management, there is a danger of rigidity in donor-induced economic policy. Given the diversity of African countries, there is a need for flexibility in donor approaches to policy reform.

Conceptual differences often arise between external agencies and African governments over the need for certain policies and over how they can be most effectively implemented and monitored. The situation is beginning to change, however, as more cognizance is taken of national circumstances when developing structural adjustment programs. This change has arisen partly from the more active role being taken by the African countries concerned. In some cases, for example, Nigeria and Zambia, donor involvement was rejected due to conflicting approaches, and subsequent relationships developed between the donor and the recipient country that were on a different basis.

Donors have influenced and continue to influence, and in some cases dominate, the policy process. An appropriate system for donor/policymaker interaction needs to be defined. What should the nature of donor involvement be? At issue is the definition of institutional development within a particular political environment. One suggestion is that external agencies work with countries to facilitate the consideration of institutional issues and the development of institutional capacity rather than imposing donor preferences for certain institutional arrangements.

Donor assistance is important in the strengthening of existing institutional capacities, particularly through the provision of resources that would strengthen the localization of training and that would more fully develop local training institutions. The development of such capacity is important for dealing with external agencies, for ensuring that African governments have the required institutional infrastructure, organizational capacity, personnel, and procedures for achieving proper integration of externally supported programs within the appropriate national policy frameworks.

The Need for More Cooperative Efforts

At issue is more than the question of structural adjustment policies. The debate is over the attitudes of donors and the values of program managers. The problem lies in the way structural adjustment was introduced and what was rational within the prevailing situation in the early 1980s. At that time there was little understanding of the impact of structural adjustment on society. In the 1990s this issue and both the economics and the feasibility of specific policies need to be examined. Success lies in the partnership that can develop, for example, between the IMF and the recipient country, and in the way that the World Bank, the UNDP, and other donors complement that partnership. African governments need programs rather than projects, and interactive action rather than episodic activity.

In the past ten years the IMF, the World Bank, and African governments have learned a great deal. The African state, not the international community, is (or should be) responsible for implementation of government policies. In the 1980s IMF policies pushed/forced governments to take certain actions that were not domestically feasible. In many cases this increased human suffering. Such outcomes do not constitute acceptable policy reform. In the 1990s there needs to be more cooperation and a better awareness of the institutional requirements for policy reform with a human face.

Structural adjustment requirements have not helped strengthen the public sector, although the reforms depend upon public sector capacity. In many countries, motivation is low, civil servants are depressed, and this poor morale has resulted in retention problems (at least as far as those with talent are concerned). Attitudes have also been affected more widely and the ever-present spirit of national service that characterized the postindependence period is long gone. Regrettably, nothing has replaced the postindependence idealism and commitment to national development.

To correct the above, African governments are now more active in national priority setting and in managing donor involvement, which is crucial to regaining ownership of the process. Such actions must also be accompanied by more efforts to allow local personnel to manage externally supported programs. Donor awareness of and commitment to these issues should be a priority of African governments and other actors concerned with the capacity building process in Africa.

Capacity Building for Policy Change

At the conclusion of the conference ten summary statements were prepared by the participants in an effort to capture and articulate the major themes surrounding capacity building efforts to support policy change and sustainability in the African context. They are as follows.

1. Capacity building is related to a complex set of human resource development issues that range from strategies of localization, training, and professionalization of the civil service, to the issue of "delocalization" of positions under structural adjustment (or for efficiency criteria).
2. Structural adjustment makes requirements on governments. Thus, there is a need for a strong and efficient state to carry out policy change and economic reforms.
3. There continues to be a role for an activist, interventionist state in the development process in a post–structural adjustment period.
4. A major issue in the structural adjustment debate is the role of the private sector and the market system as well as the appropriate balance between the public and private (including the not-for-profit) sectors.
5. Reforms often involve the introduction of task forces (as in military governments) or working groups and/or other ad hoc arrangements to solve problems. These groups can make a contribution but their institutional experience is often lost when they are dissolved without integrating their experiences into the public management system.

6. The bottleneck of policymaking and, in particular, policy reform is the policy implementation process. Attempts to avoid the difficult questions that implementation often poses can lead to the dangerous situation of choosing a policy that requires very little implementation rather than a more effective policy that demands rigorous implementation resources. Reformers thus opt for privatization rather than public-private partnerships.

7. The nature of the political process and the way that participation occurs, or does not occur, provides a framework for policymaking. Transparency and consultation are important. At issue is the question of whether or not there is a particular political framework that ensures good policy and debate about policy alternatives.

8. Donors have influenced, continue to influence, and, in same cases, dominate the policy process. An appropriate system for donor/policymaker interaction needs to be defined.

9. There are three ways to understand the policy process. Policymaking involves: legal constraints and guidelines, institutional structures and prescribed processes, and individual and group behavior. In strengthening the policy process, each component of policymaking must be addressed.

10. There are often problems of goal distortion in the policy implementation process: either through nonaction; diversion of, or lack of, resources; or through corruption, which undermines equitable access to resources. Efforts need to be made in all phases of the policy cycle to avoid such distortion.

Conclusion

In the 1950s, 1960s, and 1970s the state was seen as "developmental" with the public sector coming to dominate society. In the 1980s this view was significantly altered. Many talked about rolling back the state in terms of its areas of responsibility.

In the 1990s there is likely to be a more balanced view of the state with little discussion of either state-centric development or the abolition of the state's development role. The extremes on both ends of the ideological spectrum have been discredited. What remains is the need for appropriate models for the formulation and implementation of development policies in the public, private, and not-for-profit sectors.

There will continue to be a need to scale back on state activity in African countries. At the same time, governments must have appropriate development policies in order to plan for institutional development throughout society.

There continue to be some who accept the need for a smaller state and some who do not. This conflict is real. For many who advocate state-planned development, decentralization is often seen as an alternative to privatization. An appropriate balance between the two strategies of reform must be developed for each country within its own historical, cultural, and social context.

Policy reform needs to focus on changing the domestic private sector in Africa. Policy change must include nurturing strategies for the fledgling private sector in many African countries. These strategies must be accompanied by a serious discussion of public sector–private sector boundaries, and a serious attempt to deregulate indigenously based economic activity. For example, there is no longer any room for state policies that limit the access of private taxis to and from airports or international hotels, or that defend retail traders against the informal sector. Deregulation must not be approached from an ideological perspective, but from a task-oriented, practical, and entrepreneurial viewpoint.

Discussions of policy reform should evolve out of realistic appraisals of what the state can and cannot do, given its limited financial resources and human skills. There also needs to be a continued focus on governance and the transition from single to multiple centers of decisionmaking. Multiple centers of decisionmaking and influence require organizational capacity, institutionalized processes, and an agreed-upon definition of the nature of the decisionmaking process. The process involves the definition of roles and the extent to which they should be formalized. The nature of governance and models of decisionmaking remain controversial in many African countries. An absence of an agreement on basic principles will continue to impede the development of sustainable policies in many countries.

9

Improving Management Performance in Africa: Collaborative Intervention Models

Louis A. Picard & Michele Garrity

Donor-supported interventions have been an integral part of the development process in Africa over the past thirty years. The structural adjustment decade (1980s) of policy reform and private-sector development programs has drawn both bilateral and multilateral donors deeper into the development process of many African countries.

Given the radical changes being implemented, and the need to prepare for the post–structural adjustment period, it is important to reexamine the nature and scope of donor involvement in institution building, program management activities, and human resource development, and in what ways these activities have impacted on the performance of African managers and institutions. In particular, it is important to assess the extent to which African educational and training institutions as well as newly emerging NGOs are prepared to assume responsibility for training managers and administrators for the twenty-first century.

This chapter examines institutional development and capacity building issues within the context of donor-recipient relationships and assesses the extent to which donor-supported interventions have improved management performance. The discussion is based on our experiences with capacity building in Africa. Lessons from technical assistance activities in Guinea-Conakry, in the Southern African Development Coordination Conference (SADCC),[1] and from a World Bank institutional development project in support of management training in Southern and Western Africa inform the discussion. It is our contention that donor efforts to improve management performance in Africa have not met the challenge posed at independence. Human resource development has long been related to institutional development and sustainability,[2] but management skills, in particular, continue to be the weak link in the development policy chain. There are a number of factors that have contributed to the present situation.

First, explanations can be found in the nature of the donor-recipient relationship. Over the years, technical assistance projects have tended to be rigid and predictable. For example, the U.S. Agency for International Development's human resource development activities have relied almost exclusively on participant training tied to U.S.-based academic institutions and contracting organizations. Large numbers of short courses and certificate programs have continued to move hundreds of thousands of African participants to U.S. classrooms, despite the numerous language and logistical problems inherent in such activity. Although factors such as ideology, foreign policy, and efficiency have most certainly informed the decisions for such arrangements, they have not served the development of African educational and training institutions well.

Second, the donor-recipient relationship has evolved very little over the past thirty years. Host countries have remained the "recipients" of donor largesse. Little attention has been given to imparting donor methods, strategies, and rationales to host-country program managers in any significant or formal way. As a result, African program managers, when they are so inclined, have been forced to learn the intricacies of donor language, project documentation, and funding mechanisms on their own. The cumulative impact of this uneven relationship has often been negative and soured the best intentions of mission personnel and other field staff to establish a more equal relationship with host country counterparts. Frequent influxes of short-term consultants with narrowly focused expertise have also reinforced the unequal quality of the relationship.

Third, explanations can be found in the nature of interdonor relations, which are tenuous at best. Donors both run in packs and actively compete against one another. Once again, ideology, foreign policy concerns, and different operating styles have often mitigated against successful joint endeavors and coordination. Both institutional and human resource development have suffered from poorly coordinated donor interventions, particularly where projects and programs are long term and wide in scope.

Much attention has focused on identifying problems, designing activities, and clearing up implementation snags, but sustainable development remains elusive. The initiation of structural adjustment policies, with their emphasis on market forces, has revealed important insights about environmental factors that have a direct influence on capacity building and sustainability issues. The attention now being given to stakeholder and interest group influence in project planning activities has opened up new avenues for capacity building in the public sector. Implicit in this focus has been the need to bolster weak states while trimming away at bloated bureaucracies. An increased role for NGOs also has provided a ready source of information and expertise outside of traditional authority structures and has the potential to build capacity over a broad range of areas outside of the public sector.

At the same time, the focus on market-driven policies has highlighted the weaknesses of past institution building and human resource development strategies. The need for efficient managers, public-private partnerships, reliable systems for data collection and analysis, and multichannel information flows supports the contention that management skills are an art as well as a science. Donor interventions have not been effective at transferring the highly refined skills of analytical thinking that are so critical to the development of the systems and processes necessary for sustainable development.

Management performance in Africa has suffered accordingly from the past failures of donor initiatives to build capacity. Out of the institution-building experiences of the projects examined in this chapter, we have reviewed what has worked and what has not. Where linkages between and among donors and other host country actors were not developed, the projects suffered, and little occurred in the way of institutional and human resource development; the projects were designed and implemented in isolation. On the other hand, where linkages were recognized as important to project success, collaborative models of cooperation emerged. Inherent in the models were efforts to consider the environmental factors at work, the need to establish long-term relationships, the importance of sharing responsibilities, and the need for accountability.

In looking toward the future, a particular type of collaboration has merit. Contracting-out as a development model has a number of advantages relevant to both public and private sector activities. From a theoretical perspective, it is truly a learning process model, with many opportunities for feedback and adjustment. From a practical standpoint, it emphasizes accountability, stresses efficiency, redefines old patterns of relationships, and builds both institutional and human resource capacity in innovative ways. It also has the potential to become a reliable framework within which many types of collaborative arrangements can emerge.

The Nature of the Projects

The Performance Management Experience in SADCC

From 1984 to 1988, the Performance Management Project, through the National Association of Schools of Public Affairs and Administration (NASPAA),[3] conducted research and design work, and helped establish the Management Resource Unit (MRU) of the SADCC Regional Training Council.[4] The intervention in Southern Africa was designed to support the council and the management unit as it developed a capacity to provide assistance to regional and national management training institutions in both the public and the private sector.

Following a major research project on management training in southern Africa,[5] NASPAA responded to a request by the USAID regional mission in late 1985 to assist in the creation of the MRU and in the development of a series of pilot research and training projects on intraregional trade, transport, and agriculture.

An organizational assessment or learning process model, based on professional collaboration of African and U.S. professionals, was defined in the SADCC pilot project workplan for calendar year 1987.[6] Each of the pilot activities had three separate but interlocking activities—design, implementation, and assessment—carried out by three separate collaborative teams. In each case, a collaborative arrangement with a Southern African regional organization occurred.

The first two pilot activities involved training. One pilot on intraregional trade in SADCC was carried out in cooperation with the Institute of Development Management (IDM) in Botswana; the second pilot activity, on transport management, was done in collaboration with the National Railways of Zimbabwe. In each instance a separate assessment team examined the activity. Both assessments were frank and often critical of the activities they were examining. The third pilot on agriculture was aborted.

SADCC and the SADCC Regional Business Council

In 1988, SADCC initiated the formation of an institutional framework that would define and articulate the concerns of the regional business community to their respective governments and the various organs of SADCC.

Through a cooperative agreement with USAID/Harare, the goal was to create a regional-based institution (the SADCC Regional Business Council or SRBC) that would support and foster the development of ten national, nongovernmental trade and business-related organizations through a variety of institution-building activities. The latter included applied research on regional economic policy issues, training workshops, and information dissemination activities.

The end result of such activities would establish a smoothly functioning network of SADCC-wide trade and business-related NGOs that would support the regional business community through membership programs and services. It was also hoped that the network would foster the development of shared values and a long-term commitment to improving the region's economic development. In addition to USAID's support for a regional institution (the SRBC), the UNDP and several agencies of the European Economic Community (EEC) were also active in the region providing technical assistance to individual SRBC members.[7]

Two years after the SRBC was established, an internal study of the SRBC and its members found that many organizational development issues, such as management skills training, strategic planning and program design, and implementation and evaluation had received insufficient attention.[8] A 1992 USAID evaluation also found weak institution development. In particular, problems arose from the way in which technical assistance occurred at the various member organizations. Technical assistance had tended to follow one of two patterns: a specific set of activities was funded with support for one or more resident foreign advisers, or both operational and program monies were available with support for one or more resident advisers and successive, short-term consultants. In the latter pattern, one of the resident advisers typically assumed administrative responsibility. In either situation, training for local counterparts was usually included through on-the-job or participant training arrangements, and little or no training was provided for the executive directors or the board members of the NGOs. The limitations on organizational development under such circumstances were many. In particular, the recommendations of the internal study urged the SRBC to focus more attention on institution-building and training activities for its individual member institutions.

The Performance Management Experience in Guinea

Beginning in 1986, NASPAA, through its field office in Guinea, worked with the Ministry of Agriculture in a series of training and organizational development activities.[9] The intervention in Guinea-Conakry took an organizational development format within Guinea's

Ministry of Agriculture (formerly the Ministry of Rural Development). The goal of the project was to use organizational development techniques to increase management effectiveness.

The NASPAA intervention began with a request by the secretary-general of the then Ministry of Rural Development to assist in the organizational strengthening of the ministry. Initial design work in late 1986 proposed a series of iterative interventions with a continuous feedback process. The organizational development activity was to begin with the top management of the ministry (the secretary-general and his directors general) and work outward throughout the central ministry and eventually into the field. The process involved the ministry in defining both its own mission in the post–Sekou Touré period, and the nature of the ministry's extension services in the areas of agriculture, livestock, and fisheries.

After an initial set of activities, the project bogged down for most of calendar year 1987, with changes of personnel in both the USAID mission and in the project management team. A resident adviser was provided to the ministry in 1988; in late 1989, the USAID Guinea mission awarded NASPAA a direct contract to manage the project. As of 1993, the project continued intermittently to deliver short-term technical assistance.[10] Most of the 2.8 million dollars in the project have been consumed by administrative and overhead costs.

The World Bank UNEDIL Project

In 1985, the World Bank's Economic Development Institute (EDI), in cooperation with the UNDP and the International Labour Organisation (ILO), began the design of an institution-building project for training institutions throughout Africa (UNEDIL).[11] The UNEDIL project gave priority to the development of collaborative mechanisms between LDC institutions and individuals and organizations in the industrialized countries.[12] The purpose of the UNEDIL project was to provide support for regional training institutions, both Francophone and Anglophone, through UNEDIL-sponsored training, organizational development, research, and consultancy missions.[13] Under the project, ten to fifteen of the strongest institutions on the continent were to be provided with significant financial support and be utilized as subcontractors in training activities where appropriate. Such a practice is well developed in many parts of Latin America and Asia.

Following usual World Bank practice, the UNEDIL project took a long time to germinate. For over two years, regional seminars and workshops were held with institute representatives throughout the continent under the leadership of the EDI. Several applied research projects and a number of training activities also occurred at target institutes. In 1987, regional representatives were appointed in Gaborone, Botswana, for Anglophone Africa, and in Yaonde, Cameroon, for Francophone Africa. The project sputtered on for some five years with low levels of activity, and the resident offices were terminated in March 1993.

Separate Tracks Versus Collaborative Linkages for Training and Institutional Development

USAID in Guinea did not involve an African or Guinean institution in the ministry's organizational development project. In part the USAID decision was based on the recognition that there were no training institutions in Conakry capable of involvement in the Ministry of Agriculture project. Further, there was no discussion in Guinea that training institution capacity be created within the country.

The Guinea USAID mission, and the ministry in Guinea, could have considered linking project training activities to a Francophone regional training institution. This type of collaborative model had already been successful in the first SADCC pilot activity where institutional services were subcontracted with the IDM in Botswana and with NASPAA acting as an adviser. Although the suggestion was made to involve regional institutions between 1986 and 1987, there was no interest in the USAID Conakry mission to develop a collaborative arrangement.[14] USAID officials were leery of involving third-country or regional organizations because it would complicate the project. Instead, NASPAA involvement replicated the normal contractor/mission relationship with a host country client, with a resident adviser assisted by U.S.-based "parachute" missions put together by NASPAA in Washington.

With the project's expansion through a NASPAA direct management contract, there also might have been an attempt to formalize linkages between NASPAA (or a NASPAA subset of schools) and a West African institute, for the long-term planning and implementation of Guinea and/or regional activities.[15]

The Guinea project lingered on for over five years without significant program activity. The project continued because the USAID mission needed to expend funds regardless of the lack of program performance in the activity. Through the NASPAA intervention in the Ministry of Agriculture, the Guinea USAID mission had hoped to placate a Ministry of Agriculture that was cut out of major project support when sectoral funding under structural adjustment caused the termination of agricultural-based rural development projects in 1986.[16]

Despite the initial collaborative successes, the SADCC/MRU was stillborn, lasting little more than a year as an experimental activity. The project did not meet its goals because it failed to develop long-term collaborative linkages with other host country and regional actors. The absence of such linkages also meant that the project never developed significant domestic institutional capacity. Lack of donor support for the project also caused problems. For example, the SADCC/MRU project was battered by a USAID regional mission (Southern Africa) that changed its regional priorities three times in fifteen months.[17] After abandoning the MRU project, USAID officials blamed the MRU administrator (on the job less than eighteen months) for the failure of the project.

The World Bank/UNEDIL project began about the same time that NASPAA began its intervention in Guinea and in SADCC. However, despite the close proximity of interests, few bilateral donors became involved in UNEDIL activities. As a result, the bilateral training projects evolved in separate tracks from the World Bank effort at institutional strengthening.

Although the UNEDIL project did not link up with bilateral training efforts, advocates of collaboration between local institutions and donors did exist at the time. Within the West African region, and particularly in the Francophone area, there had been discussion by USAID of an increased emphasis on management training using West African regional institutions under the UNEDIL project. Some USAID officials in the region have argued that this should be the case with regard to research and consultancy training as well.[18]

Approaches to Collaboration at the SRBC

Given the SRBC's private-sector development focus, the organization was deluged with offers of technical assistance from a host of bilateral, multilateral, and private aid agencies. Most of these offers, however, consisted of short-term assistance provided by teams of foreign-based consultants. Following the SRBC's internal assessment study and a strategic planning workshop for the members, the SRBC pursued a number of creative approaches to build capacity through linkages with other NGOs.

One such approach involved a collaborative arrangement with the U.S.-based Center for International Private Enterprise (CIPE) to improve overall management performance using CIPE's expertise in training programs for nonprofit managers.[19] Beginning with an initial workshop involving regional business-related NGO managers, the SRBC planned to collaborate with CIPE in establishing a Southern Africa–based management training program.

Another collaborative approach focused on the development of an SRBC-sponsored chamber of commerce exchange program. The program's goal was to build institutional linkages between individual NGOs across the region and the more successful NGOs, providing personnel and technical assistance to less developed NGOs. A secondary goal was to strengthen the consulting and marketing capacity of the program's participants.

A third approach was aimed at developing regional consultants. Through collaborative partnerships, the SRBC would contract with local expertise in the areas of trade, investment, and management for the design and delivery of special programs or packages of services that would be marketed to other NGOs in the region.[20]

These and other innovative approaches tried at the SRBC, however, were never vigorously supported by the USAID regional mission in Harare. Nor did the SRBC's parent organization, the SADCC, fully support its initiatives. Both USAID and SADCC personnel failed to understand both the uniqueness of the SRBC experiment and the nature of the institutional constraints the SRBC faced in the region. In particular, institutional and human resource capacity issues were ignored by the mission and SADCC. As a result of the low priority given to capacity issues, all the SRBC members were viewed as viable organizations capable of fully implementing and sustaining SRBC-sponsored programs directed at the regional business community. In practice, many of the SRBC members could not meet the demands of planning, coordinating, or implementing activities.

The SRBC was slow to recognize that weak institutional and human resource capacity was bogging down its activities. Once the dimensions of the problems became apparent, however, the SRBC focused more efforts on institution-building activities directed at the member organizations rather than an exclusive focus on business community–related activities. Support for the former, however, was challenged repeatedly by the donor and misunderstood by SADCC headquarters, resulting in endless revisions to the SRBC workplan and needless delays in actually carrying out activities. In this environment, many of the collaborative approaches adopted by the SRBC were never fully implemented, and capacity issues continued to plague the SRBC. USAID support for the SRBC terminated in 1992 after less than two years of support.

Collaborative Models and Institutional Development

There are several observations that can be made about NASPAA[21] and the Performance Management Project and from its unfulfilled synergy with the UNEDIL project. They apply equally as well to the SADCC-SRBC project. A comparison of activities can provide lessons for future management development efforts.

Capacity building efforts need to avoid the creation of separate tracks for educational and training efforts and institution-building activity. All training efforts should involve local or regional training institutions. In the Guinea project, no attempt was made in the first three years of the project to involve either a Guinean or West African regional training institution in the activity. Rather, the project was managed by the Washington-based NASPAA with a coordinator resident in Conakry. From an institutional development perspective, this may have been a major flaw in the design of the project.

In addition to the other problems of the NASPAA/MRU project, the absence of interdonor coordination had a significant and negative impact on this complex experiment. An effort to involve the multilateral UNEDIL project would have been useful to USAID interventions in both SADCC and Guinea. The absence of multilateral and bilateral donor coordination weakened both efforts. As both examples show, USAID and other donors require continual prodding to insure that all of their management support activities are collaborative and are based on a learning process mode of operation.

A successful donor intervention requires the development of viable collaborative linkages between and among host country stakeholders and technical assistance delivery mechanisms. There must be something in it for all players or the effort will fail. Donor coordination, though difficult, also needs to be aggressively pursued.

Between 1979 and 1989, NASPAA and the Performance Management Project tried, with only mixed success, to develop a professional collaboration model in a number of their field-based research and training and organizational development activities.[22] Moreover, NASPAA tried to work with an organizational development and learning process model that included both on-going and independent assessments of its activities, and a step-by-step adjustable planning approach.[23] Such a collaborative mode and its learning process model of organizational development may be a useful model not only for the USAID but for other donors as well. The two interventions by NASPAA under a USAID Cooperative Agreement[24] illustrate the various approaches such a model offers and highlight the problems that can arise when donors play a significant role in institutional development activities.

There is little institutional memory in the donor-client relationship. In the SADCC-SRBC project, it is ironic to note that two years into the project neither the SRBC nor USAID was aware of the NASPAA-SADCC/MRU project, even though the USAID mission in Harare funded both activities and the first MRU pilot activity involved interregional trade, an area of interest to the SRBC. Linkages between the MRU and the SRBC were virtually nonexistent. Although personnel from the Regional Training Council had expressed repeated interest in meeting and working with SRBC personnel, this received little interest from USAID personnel, and the SRBC relied on other organizations for expertise, notably outside the region. In addition, USAID personnel did not support or facilitate the development of linkages with other regional actors.

Despite the many donors already working with the ten members of the SRBC, efforts to coordinate donor activities fell on deaf ears. Further, despite the SRBC-CIPE initiative to establish a regional-based management training program, no local training institutions were brought into the discussions. Rather, lacking time and with very little support from the USAID office for the activity, the SRBC sponsored a scaled-down, poorly organized one-time workshop.

Given the context of an increased emphasis on third-country training, and training institution development for both the private and public sectors, there are a number of lessons that can be learned from these experiences. The present focus on training for the private sector, and for public sector support of market-based economic activities, is likely to prove critical to the institutional development of regional and national-based organizations.[25] Central to any complementarity that could develop between such multilateral projects as UNEDIL and bilateral donor training activities supporting public-private partnerships are institutional development efforts that are targeted at key regional and national-level training organizations. Given the current trends, it is reasonable to expect that any new human resource development projects in Africa in the 1990s are likely to have a major institutional development component.

Yet our project examples provide little evidence of support for institutional development among U.S. technical assistance officials. In the past decade, USAID in West Africa has shown little interest in institutional development within Africa in general and within the Francophone region more specifically. The UNEDIL project was underutilized as an institutional development mechanism. Moreover, as the United States moves toward private sector development, traditional techniques involving U.S. contractors and U.S.-based participant training remain the hallmarks of technical assistance. This continues to be the case in spite of the failure of these techniques to build capacity within the public sector in Africa. Interventions such as that occurring in the Guinea project continue to operate in isolation from other, similar interventions and from the indigenous institutional base that needs to be a natural part of the intervention process. Participant training continues throughout Francophone Africa in spite of the difficulties in trying to bring Americans to West Africa to work in French or to train West Africans in French in the United States—a participant training practice that goes back to the mid-1960s.[26]

Discussions of Africa-based (as opposed to U.S.-based) research, design, and training activities reinforce arguments made in earlier chapters that there is no substitute for the twin strategies of institutional development and sustainability for improving the management effectiveness of African states. In the early 1990s, donor-supported interventions are in danger of losing much of their long-term impact, whether the purpose is training, organizational development, or applied research. Whether the target is the public or the private sector, no long-term national or regional institutional capacity will develop if indigenous education and training institutions are not involved. Further, it is not unreasonable to expect that training institution development and organizational development activities can successfully run on parallel tracks or that synergistic efforts can be achieved with multiple donors pursuing common goals through uncoordinated strategies. Only program managers in LDCs can ensure that the donor/contractor focus is on transferring the capacity for organizational development to local or regional organizations rather than relying on externally based organizational development contracts or noniterative management training activities.[27] There is a negative influence running though much of the technical assistance activity for human resource development including such areas as: overseas participant training (both long and short-term); discrete, noniterative, and noninstitutional in-country training seminars; and externally managed organizational development activity. Each of these activities lacks the critical institution-building component that is essential to sustainability.[28]

The Limits of Collaboration

It is fairly easy to see with hindsight the need to develop more collaborative modes of intervention. But it is important to note there must be realistic and pragmatic mechanisms available for achieving such goals. To be truly effective, these mechanisms must fit the fragile institutional environment in Africa. In particular, the host of problems that plague African education and training institutions must be addressed. In order to understand how management development can occur, we need to examine the institutional requirements of African education and training organizations.[29]

The weak link in most education and training institutions in Africa is internal management, particularly financial management. The World Bank/UNEDIL project could have complemented donor-funded projects (such as USAID's efforts in SADCC) in its support for internal management capacity. Indeed, internal management was to be a major focus of intervention in the UNEDIL project. This is not an area where the UNEDIL project has made great strides. Internal management is a sensitive area to LDC program managers and policymakers. Nonetheless, it is an organizational weakness that needs to be recognized and addressed. There are a number of potential subcomponents to this issue that were due to be addressed in the UNEDIL project. These were strategic planning, faculty governance, motivation, and financial management.

Strategic planning. A commitment to strategic planning and market analysis on the part of management training organizations was seen as fundamental to the success of the World Bank/UNEDIL project. Complementary donor support to work with these organizations in developing long-term strategic plans could enhance an institution's performance and regularize its basis of externally generated revenue. Such efforts are particularly important in light of donor interests in private sector development.

Faculty governance. Another recurring problem has been that of institutional self-management.[30] Many African training and education institutions have political or civil service appointees as directors, many of whom lack an appropriate background in training and education issues. Without a background in such issues the potential for a misunderstanding of staff motivation and a lack of sensitivity to demands is greatly increased, particularly among those staff educated in a nonhierarchical teaching faculty system in North America or Western Europe. A breakthrough on the issue of staff or faculty governance that is culturally appropriate would be a major contribution to the institutional development of such organizations.

Motivation. The issue of motivation is central to the promotion of applied research and consultancy. In light of Maslow's hierarchy of needs[31] in the depressed conditions of many LDC educational and training institutions, it is basic human needs that predominate most African environments. For this reason, the recognition of an individual's research and consultancy contribution inevitably is linked to financial reward. The issue is not only money for money's sake. Rather there must be acknowledgement that retained consultancy fees and merit salary increases also contribute to ego enhancement.

Training institutions in Africa often suffer from two extremes. At the one extreme, institutions have no arrangements to reward productive staff members who generate applied research and consultancy work. At the other extreme exists the problem of "runaway" consultancy. In the latter, the staff neglects training, research, and materials development work in order to pursue more lucrative consultancies. One approach to "runaway" consultancies is the introduction of a formula for sharing within the institution.[32]

Financial management. Without a sound program of financial management reform, training institutions are not likely to approach financial self-sufficiency. Internal financial management problems were given high priority in the design of the UNEDIL project. USAID, through its support of institutional development activities, could have complemented the World Bank project in this area. NASPAA, for example, in its support of the SADCC Management Resource Unit, became involved in three sets of internal management activities through its subcontracting relationships with training institutes. The activities included institute billing, financial reporting, and consultant expense submission. By the time NASPAA completed its cooperative agreement, it had considerable insight into the internal financial management of a number of management training institutes and support organizations.

Collaborative Models Between and Among Donors

The examples can also be used to examine another aspect of capacity building that needs to be addressed when considering collaborative intervention models—the successful coordination of multiple, complementary donor activity. Interdonor collaboration remains an elusive and neglected aspect of effective capacity building efforts in Africa. For example, although there was a great deal of potential complementarity within SADCC between USAID support, German Technical Cooperation (GTZ), and European Community support for human resource development, this was not effectively exploited, even though all three provided support for the SADCC regional training council and its management resource unit. Neither was there any attempt to involve the World Bank/UNEDIL project in the development of SADCC management training institutes.[33]

In spite of SADCC's eight years of existence, the UNEDIL project neither treated the SADCC states as a separate subregional unit nor used the SADCC Regional Training Council as a mechanism to coordinate the World Bank project in the subregion. There was no effective donor coordination on management training between the UNEDIL project and the bilateral donors in SADCC. Interdonor coordination between the World Bank and USAID as well as other technical assistance organizations (such as those in Canada or Germany) has been difficult at best since USAID began its support of the SADCC Regional Training Council in the early 1980s.

After 1988, the absence of interdonor cooperation, management weakness, vacillation within the government of Swaziland, and lethargy on the part of USAID officials in the Southern African region led German technical assistance to take the lead role in the MRU Unit activity. U.S. involvement in human resource development in SADCC was diverted to the private sector, where eventually the USAID-funded SADCC Regional Business Council emerged with no linkages to ongoing training programs in the region.

Collaboration Through Contracting-Out

Strategies for institutional development and human resource development must be pursued simultaneously. The strategies must also be pursued in ways that will promote the utilization of local institutions and that will build capacity both within local institutions and within the communities they are to serve. One effective mechanism involves collaboration based on a contracting-out mode between donors and key regional and national-level training institutions and/or NGOs.

One contracting-out scenario involves developing and utilizing appropriate regional institutions that could replicate and perhaps eventually replace the contractor capacity in U.S.-style participant training and U.S.-contracted design and implementation activities. A contracting-out model involving regional institutions or associations of institutions would bring participants to a regional center for management training rather than send participants to the

United States.[34] The coming to power of a nonracial government in South Africa will significantly increase the pool of African education and training institutions that can deliver management training and make the model even more attractive. To ensure management performance, internal USAID evaluations could place equal emphasis on both training and institutional development in assessments of the management training activity.

Hands-on training is all that training institutions in Africa currently provide. Consequently, little capacity exists for applied research and consultancy. Whatever their advantages, short courses, fellowships, and networking activities alone will not provide African training institutions with the kind of professional experience that meeting the demands of a contract or subcontract will provide. The primary need of management training institutions in Africa is donor support in the development of an applied research and consultancy capacity rather than support for training activity alone.[35]

Contracting-out mechanisms also allow for less intrusive methods of internal management strengthening. For example, organizations contracting with a donor or a prime contractor would not be paid until the task is completed and the billing and expense reports are completed correctly. Further, contracting allows for an auditing mechanism based on deliverables that is not politically feasible in donor/client relationships. Support for financial management based upon these "on the job needs" would be appropriate whether the work is being done in the public or the private sector; the model is replicable over a variety of situations and among many types of donors. Pursuing enhanced management performance through a contractor/subcontractor mode rather than a donor-client mode changes both perceptions and the practical needs of capacity building through its focus on accountability and transparency.[36]

The model proposed above explicitly recognizes that a central component in developing training institution capacity lies in the understanding that bilateral and multilateral donors are potentially major "clients" of African training and research institutions.[37] Through the contracting-out mode of operation, donors can accomplish a number of objectives: (1) they contribute to the basic financial support of the organization; (2) a sound, high-quality product in research, organizational development, or training is developed and delivered; (3) the donor as client maintains the right to evaluate (and audit) the organization's performance of contractual obligations in ways that are not possible through the normal technical-assistance relationship; and (4) through the financial reporting process, the donor or prime contractor can provide the organization with feedback on its internal financial management system.[38]

Along these same lines, assistance could also be provided for the development of consortiums of institutions (both U.S. and African), which would then compete for contracts (using the request for proposal process in USAID parlance). African consortiums for project design, implementation, and evaluation activities would contribute significantly to an institutional capacity in training and research. Another mechanism for promoting local institutional capacity would be a requirement by donors that there be local institution representation in international competitive bids (or set-aside projects). These could occur along the lines of the Eight-A firm requirements in the United States.

Work within SADCC under the Performance Management Project and the SRBC experiment provided a major, if brief, opportunity for innovative and flexible collaboration between USAID and African training institutions and host country professionals. The SADCC Regional Business Council experience had the potential to extend the collaborative concept to include the rapidly growing NGO sector. These experiences are not unique to the SADCC region, and the collaborative model should be viewed as a viable alternative over a wide variety of circumstances and geographic locales.

Conclusion

African institutional capacity is out of sync with that in many parts of Asia and Latin America. This, in part, reflects the chronic nature of Africa's economic crisis. Institutional incapacity may also be a partial cause of the crisis.

The Performance Management Project throughout its ten-year history conveyed a message of "professional collaboration" between practitioners in LDCs and their U.S. counterparts; professional collaborators should be an integral component of all technical assistance interventions in the 1990s and beyond.[39] However, collaboration does not come naturally, and unless it is built into the competitive bidding process, it will get scant attention from USAID and other donors and contractors.

Donor-supported interventions for management effectiveness work best when based upon an institution-building model. This model is not put forward because African educational and training institutions are strong. They are not. If anything, educational and training capacity has decreased since independence in much of Africa, which has had a negative impact on public sector performance, and now threatens to undermine the management performance of the private sector (including NGO activity) in many African countries.

The failure to address institutional development issues in the 1990s inevitably will result in a continual spiral of foreign-based training activities and a lack of internal institutional capacity for human resource development in Africa. This is an issue that can best be monitored by the LDC policymaker and the program manager. It is in the interest of the donor recipient, not the donor, that institutional development occur. Left to their own devices, many donors will continue to rely on externally managed participant training, in-country training, and organizational development activities that have characterized much of the post–World War II period. They do so because U.S.-managed activities are relatively efficient and because they move money quickly.

Many of the institutional development issues discussed in this chapter, such as internal management, involve matters of extreme sensitivity. No doubt, many are beyond the scope of donor interest and the donor system as it now exists.[40] Yet, institutional development remains one of the pillars of USAID policy, and institutional capacity building is crucial to developing successful strategies for public-private partnerships that are currently being pursued. It is an issue that will not go away.

The absence of linkages between the NASPAA interventions in Western and Southern Africa and the World Bank/UNEDIL project, and between the SRBC and these actors, also illustrates the need for complementarity of donor activity. Donors both run in packs in terms of policy priorities and compete with one another for the attention of LDC program managers. It is this competition that may allow local managers to set technical assistance priorities.

The 1990s are likely to see a new paradigm in technical assistance. Now that many donors have declared that the "war" to upgrade the public sector has been won (or lost, depending on one's perspective), attention has turned to the battle to upgrade the private sector in Africa. Support for the private sector will undoubtedly face the same issues of donor complementarity and institutional development that have challenged public sector support for the last thirty years.

Professional collaborative relationships, and especially contracting-out as a development model, provide a number of interesting and potentially highly successful activities aimed at adapting current practices. As the examples in this chapter have shown, there are numerous approaches to collaborative arrangements among both the traditional training and education institutions and their newly emerging counterparts in the not-for-profit sector. Together these institutions offer a diversity of vehicles for upgrading management performance in Africa.

Notes

1. The Southern African Development Coordination Conference (SADCC) is a regional development organization based in Botswana, comprising the member governments of Angola, Botswana, Lesotho, Malawi, Mozambique, Namibia, Swaziland, Tanzania, Zambia, and Zimbabwe. In 1992 the regional body was renamed the Southern African Development Council (SADC). Given the time period covered in this chapter we will continue to use the more familiar name.

2. See for example, Joseph Eaton, ed., *Institution Building and Development: From Concepts to Application* (Beverly Hills, Calif.: Sage Publications, 1972).

3. Between 1979 and 1989, NASPAA comanaged the Performance Management Project through a cooperative agreement with USAID. The purpose of the project, through its applied research and strategic interventions, was to develop new knowledge about the management needs and institutional requirements for public and private sector organizations. During the ten-year period, NASPAA consultants carried out research and sponsored interventions in organizational development and management training in Africa, Asia, and Latin America.

4. USAID was already providing support to the SADCC Regional Training Council (RTC), under which the Management Resource Unit (MRU) was to be located. The RTC was a representative board made up of delegates from each of the then nine SADCC countries. Its administrative secretariat was supposed to be the Swaziland Department of Economic Planning and Statistics. However, the Swazi government would not allocate personnel for the RTC. As a result, USAID decided to try to provide administrative capacity by financing a subunit, the MRU, which was outside of the Swaziland civil service establishment. Technical assistance personnel were divided between the RTC and the MRU, a decision that had a negative impact on both the organizational capacity to grant assistance to educational and training institutions and on the long-term sustainability of the activity.

5. The research project used the critical incidents method. The project report recommended, among other things, the creation of a Management Development Resource Center (MADREC) as part of a projected major U.S., EC, and German intervention in support of private-sector and public-sector management training in SADCC. The USAID-funded MRU was a scaled-down version of the MADREC concept. *Improving Management in Southern Africa* (Washington, D.C.: National Association of Schools of Public Affairs and Administration, July 1, 1985). The research director of the project was Prof. John Montgomery of Harvard University. One of the authors of this chapter (Picard) served on the research team.

6. "Workplan and Schedule of Activities," Management Resource Unit, April 1987–April 1988 (Mbabane, Swaziland: National Association of Schools of Public Affairs and Administration, March 1987). The term "assessment," in the organizational development sense, should not be confused with "evaluation" in the donor sense of the word. As defined by

the donors, "evaluation" is a midpoint or terminal action that is separate from on-going project activity.

NASPAA advocated a frank assessment of organizational and/or training institution capabilities that occurred within the context of the on-going implementation of an activity. As such, judgment was not made of the overall project, but each activity was to be assessed as part of a planning adjustment process that would allow activities to move from one stage of the project to the next (as in the Guinea project) or from one pilot to the next (as in the SADCC activities). Both programmatic and administrative (for example, financial management and reporting) assessments were components of the process.

7. The UNDP was involved in Zambia and Angola and was negotiating with the Government of Tanzania to provide organizational development support for a newly created national chamber of commerce. In Zimbabwe, Botswana, Lesotho, and Swaziland, chambers of commerce and trade-related NGOs were receiving various levels of support for organizational development and institution-building activities from USAID and from German and Scandinavian aid agencies. Except for USAID in Botswana and the proposed UNDP project in Tanzania, most of the technical assistance projects were small in size and of limited duration. Accordingly, the impact of such projects was negligible given the low levels of institutional development of many of the grantees.

8. Michele Garrity, *Needs Assessment Study for the SADCC Regional Business Council* (Gaborone: SADCC Regional Business Council, April 9, 1991).

9. Activities were initially carried out under the Cooperative Agreement between NASPAA and USAID's Bureau of Science and Technology, the USAID mission in Conakry, and the Government of Guinea. Later, NASPAA became a contractor to USAID Conakry for the project.

10. In March 1993, the project was put out for competitive bid.

11. "Proposal for SADCC Regional Program in Management Training; Pre-MADREC Phase" (Mbabane, Swaziland: National Association of Schools of Public Affairs and Administration, July 11, 1986) and "Description of UNDP/EDI Project to Strengthen Training Institutions in Africa" (Washington, D.C.: World Bank, n.d.). The UNDP/EDI Project was called the "UNEDIL Project" in the field, the acronym coming from the first two initials of UNDP, EDI, and ILO. The project took four years to develop and still is criticized for doing more talking than implementing. The project's field operations were terminated inconclusively in March 1993.

12. The World Bank, in its African Capacity Building Initiative program for sub-Saharan Africa, also pledged support for the institutional development of management training institutions as part of their strategy to strengthen NGO management, professional associations, consultancy firms, and policy analysis units. *The African Capacity Building Initiative: Toward Improved Policy Analysis Development* (Washington, D.C.: World Bank, 1991).

13. Lee Roberts, *The Policy Environment of Management Development Institutions in Anglophone Africa: Problems and Prospects for Reform* (Washington, D.C.: World Bank, 1990).

14. One of the authors of this chapter (Picard), as director of the NASPAA/AID project, helped to design the Guinea activity during this period.

15. The Centre Africain d'Etudes Superieures en Gestion (CESAG) in

Senegal (among others) might have been an appropriate candidate for such a linkage, given its academic level and its involvement in the World Bank UNEDIL upgrading project.

16. This statement is based on discussions one of the authors (Picard) had with officials in the USAID mission in Conakry in 1987.

17. Further, the regional mission found it easier to move money by buying hardware for transport projects in Mozambique than to invest the time and effort in the painful and slow process of human resource development and capacity building.

18. Personal communications with one of the authors (Picard) during trips to Senegal, Ivory Coast, Togo, Central African Republic, Congo-Brazzaville, and Zaire in March 1987.

19. CIPE is an affiliate of the U.S. Chamber of Commerce and provides grants to a wide range of NGOs in less developed countries, particularly for institutional development activities. In Latin America, CIPE's collaborative efforts with NGOs evolved into a local training institute offering both practical and theoretical coursework on the management and operation of chambers of commerce.

20. For example, trade promotion programs involve a number of discrete activities such as sectoral studies, feasibility studies, buyer/seller meetings, and overseas and regional trade missions. Taken together, these activities constitute a package or program of services and products that can be marketed to trade and investment-related organizations.

21. NASPAA and USAID might have better publicized its mode of operation within the international donor community and within Africa. At this point far too little is known about the NASPAA/Performance Management mode of operation, particularly in Africa. During the ten years of its existence the project was little understood by most USAID missions in the field, and it often became seen as little more than a contracting mechanism to move awkward amounts of money without the necessity of a competitive bidding process.

22. These activities included the 1984 SADCC Management Needs study, the University of Pittsburgh Francophone Management Seminars, NASPAA's support for SADCC management training activities, and its organizational development work in Guinea (as well as similar activities in Latin America and Asia).

23. See Derick W. Brinkerhoff, *Improving Development Program Performance: Guidelines for Managers* (Boulder, Colo.: Lynne Rienner Publishers, 1991), pp. 27–62, for a discussion of this. The ideas behind the learning process model go back more than fifty years as bottom up or action learning. However, it was David Korten, working under the Ford Foundation and later NASPAA, who popularized the term "learning process" in development management. See David Korten, "Community Organization and Rural Development: A Learning Process Approach," *Public Administration Review*, vol. 40, no. 5, pp. 480–511.

24. The Development Program Management Center (DPMC) of the U.S. Department of Agriculture was also a co-operant.

25. Oral interview, USAID Regional Human Resource Development Officer, REDSO, Abidjan, Ivory Coast.

26. These programs should now be phased out. It is significant that the Scandinavian countries, recognizing the language barriers, have largely stopped bringing participants to Scandinavia for training. Rather, support is given for training within a recipient country or within the region, with third-

country training in an English-speaking country an alternative for higher-level training. The Rural Development Center at Holte in Denmark was closed in the mid-1970s for this reason. As Japan increases its foreign aid to LDCs it is beginning to address similar issues in its technical assistance policy.

27. Morgan and Duffau categorically pointed out the limits of measuring any impact of the discrete training activity: "In a short seminar or workshop with rather general goals it is unlikely that much more than opinion and modest learning can be measured, unless the trainee returns for several iterations which could provide longitudinal data for the assessment of behavioral change, or even organizational effects." E. Philip Morgan and Jean Marie Duffau, "Institutional Management Improvement: The Francophone Development Management Seminars in the Central African Republic" (paper submitted to the National Association of Schools of Public Affairs and Administration, September 1986).

28. The plea for institution building was made by William J. Siffin, "Two Decades of Public Administration in Developing Countries," *Public Administration Review*, vol. 36, no. 1 (January–February 1976), pp. 61–71.

29. Many training institutes are actually QUANGOs (quasi-nongovernmental organizations) in the British parlance because they have linkages with governments.

30. See, for example, Kamala Choudhry, "Strategies for Institutionalizing Public Management Education: The Indian Experience," in *Education and Training for Public Sector Management in Developing Countries*, ed. Lawrence D. Stifel, Joseph Black, and James S. Coleman (New York: Working Papers of the Rockefeller Foundation, April 1978), pp. 101–110.

31. Abraham H. Maslow, *Toward a Psychology of Being* (New York: D. Van Nostrand Company, 1968), pp. 21–43.

32. An appropriate formula might be 50 percent of fees shared up to a certain number of days (possibly two to three days a month). After that, 100 percent of consultancies would revert to the institution. A subcontracting arrangement with an institution might include such a "conditionality."

33. It should have been possible for the RTC (and its donor sponsors) and the MRU to work closely with the World Bank/UNEDIL project in developing a formal linkage arrangement with EDI and a regional institution in a third pilot activity on agricultural management or applied research training.

In spite of the close proximity of the NASPAA project and the UNEDIL project in Washington (and the personal relationships which project managers of the two projects had with each other in the United States and in Africa), no linkages developed between the UNEDIL project and the NASPAA Guinea Project or with the SADCC Management Resource Unit in Swaziland.

34. In Francophone Africa, these centers could include Dakar, Senegal; Lomé, Togo; or Abidjan, Côte d'Ivoire. In Anglophone Africa, these could include Nairobi, Kenya; Arusha, Tanzania; Harare, Zimbabwe; or, in the future, Johannesburg, South Africa. Through a buy-in to the UNEDIL project, USAID missions would then have had a mechanism to utilize region-based, third-country training within Western and Southern Africa.

35. The 1984 NASPAA study, *Improving Management in Southern Africa* (Washington, D.C.: National Association of Schools of Public Affairs and Administration, July 1, 1985), makes this point. It should be noted that donor pressure for "training activities" remains very strong. In spite of the

NASPAA study, the USAID missions in Harare and Mbabane resisted the idea of a nontraining pilot project, opting instead for pilot projects with traditional formal training seminars.

36. NASPAA, under the Performance Management Project, operated in the subcontracting mode in its SADCC activities. Subcontracting arrangements were negotiated with the IDM in the first pilot, and similar contractual arrangements were developed by SADCC's Management Resource Unit with the National Railways of Zimbabwe, the Management Services Board, and the Eastern and Southern African Management Institute (ESAMI) in the second pilot training project (January–February 1988). NASPAA's collaboration with the Central American Institute of Business (INCAE) also offers another example of this kind of collaboration.

Donors in the 1990s are likely to continue to support training needs assessment, organizational development, the delivery of training seminars, and mounting of project design, evaluation, or other applied research activities. Whenever feasible and for institutional development purposes, subcontracting arrangements between donors and U.S.-based contractors and regional or national institutions in Africa should occur. These institutions, rather than U.S. universities, should be the primary beneficiaries of this type of service delivery contract. The latter could be utilized in an advisory or primary research capacity in support of the strengthening of the regional and national institutes through linkage arrangements. In an expanded "professional collaboration" model, partnership arrangements with local institutions for the mounting of teams could include both members from "core" (that is, World Bank–targeted) institutions in Africa as well as members from the United States or Western Europe as appropriate.

37. An earlier version of this model was presented in Louis A. Picard, *Report on Strengthening Management Institutes in Africa* (Pittsburgh: International Management Development Institute, December 11, 1988). This report was funded by and presented to the Technical Cooperation Project of NASPAA under the auspices of USAID's Performance Management Project.

38. Interestingly, in spite of the fact that the UNEDIL project focuses in part on internal management concerns, the donor role/responsibility as a "client" has not been directly addressed within EDI/UNEDIL project activities.

39. This is particularly true for African training institutions. Without professional collaboration, program development, faculty support efforts, and, most important, internal management concerns, will rightly be seen as highly intrusive by the faculty and administration of management training institutes.

40. It may be worth noting that for the ten years of its existence, the Performance Management Project impacted, if only in a limited way, both the theory and practice of development management in many of the areas discussed in this chapter. Unfortunately, the project has rarely received the appropriate recognition for its contribution that it deserves (as well as criticism for its institutional development "failures"). This lack of recognition is largely because project managers did not adequately disseminate the findings of their applied research.

10

Institutional Development Revisited

Michele Garrity & Louis A. Picard

Africa is subject to stereotypes. There is a sameness to the images of "tropical gangsters" and greedy expatriates, ethnic conflict and the failure of the African state.[1] With military coups, ethnic-based civil wars, and the idiosyncrasies of dictatorships on the left and right, there is much to be depressed about. And yet, Africa is made up of over fifty states; some, such as Nigeria and Ethiopia, are very large, and others, such as the Gambia and Swaziland, are microstates. Although none are NICs and can match the progress of some countries in Latin America, there is a diversity to their economic condition and the ability of the state to make and implement policy that belies much of the conventional wisdom about the continent. The chapters in this book have presented that diversity.

In this chapter we look at patterns of reform as a change strategy and the interaction between reform processes and the domestic policy environment. We conclude with a discussion of some strategies for policymaking and policy implementation that may lead to more efficient and effective development policies in Africa.

Policy Reform and Governance

Developing societies face a set of issues that relate to governance—the institutions and processes of government—and the way in which multiple centers of decisionmaking are promoted. Addressing governance issues is part of the policy reform process because structural adjustment interventions are almost always accompanied by political reforms. Effective political communication is at the heart of efforts to create multiple centers of decisionmaking. Without improved information flows and mechanisms to ensure feedback and political and economic accountability, effective governance cannot be achieved. The key to success in these efforts lies in a commitment to institution building both within government and in society as a whole.

Constitutional Reform and the Policy Process

In the countries analyzed in our case studies, constitutional reforms have occurred or are occurring in the one-party states (Zambia, Tanzania, Kenya) and in military regimes (Nigeria and Ghana). Botswana alone has maintained a formal democratic process since independence. Promoting multiple levels of decisionmaking has involved strengthening legislatures and interest organizations and introducing multipartyism. In all of these countries efforts at democratic governance are incomplete.

Attempts at introducing pluralism through the development of multiple centers of influence and decisionmaking as well as various attempts at decentralization are fragile. Policymakers have been challenged both to discover and to correct the true causes of institutional weakness and capacity. Throughout Africa, there has been lack of sustained political will to move beyond cosmetic changes. Among our case studies, Ghana and Nigeria, in particular, have witnessed a succession of government—military and civilian—that have reinterpreted reform mandates for their own purposes.

In Tanzania, after the 1967 Arusha Declaration, the party and party ideology were used to control the policy process, with government assuming the role of implementor. However, both party and government officials lacked the necessary skills and talent to make and implement policy. With the introduction of economic and political reforms after 1985, the party was relegated to reigning over the policy process, rather than making policy, as government officials and technocrats worked ever more closely with international lending agencies in implementing structural adjustment. Even with the move to a multiparty state there has been little involvement from NGOs in the policy process.

In one-party Zambia, a more integrated approach to policymaking was adopted, with government bureaucrats holding overlapping memberships in party organs. Zambian ideology did not call for the same kind of party dominance that had been sought in Tanzania, though, as in Tanzania the government assumed the role of implementor. Although the machinery of government typified the bureaucratic model, the implementation of policies was hindered and mediated by political interference, nepotism, corruption, and lack of competent personnel. The party was weaker in purpose in Zambia than was the case in Tanzania, but stronger in terms of articulating the economic interests of the organizational elites in both government and party. Elections for a new government in 1991 have done little to address these fundamental capacity problems.

Policymaking in Kenya has been dominated by the executive, where the president and the cabinet have ruled supreme, and the legislature was reduced to a reactive role. Kenya has long been characterized by a weak party system[2] and President Moi's preemptive style of decisionmaking and his long reign has marginalized the KANU role. Authoritarian rule and ethnic tensions continue to permeate Kenyan society.

The role of the Kenya bureaucracy has not been insignificant in the policy process and was further aided by legislation in the early 1970s that allowed civil servants to engage in private enterprise activities. Their influence, combined with that of foreign private investors and resident foreign donor advisers, resulted in development policies that were technocratic, but which in large measure closed the policy process to nongovernmental organizations and grassroots participation.

Ghana's political leaders early on lost ownership of the policy process. Both political instability and economic deterioration resulted in a mass exodus of indigenous professionals. Successive governments came to power with little interest in participatory styles of decisionmaking. Although the situation has greatly improved with the introduction of an economic recovery program, the coming to power of the PNDC military government, and the subsequent transition to civil rule, much still remains to be done to institutionalize and open up the policy process to civil society.

In Nigeria, a federally based system has produced a three-tiered structure in which competing interests among local, state, and federal officials have proved difficult to mediate over the years. This problem has been compounded by alternative patterns of civilian and military rule and by the policies of successive governments, which have tended to modify both government structures and processes to reflect prevailing priorities. Out of these circumstances there has emerged a powerful bureaucracy—anonymous, class based, and with strong ties to elements of the business community, which exerts considerable influence on the policy process.

Botswana, at first glance, seems to have escaped the problems of governance. With a relatively efficient state and a set of pragmatic economic policies, it has the highest economic growth rate in Africa. A closer look, however, reveals similar weaknesses in Botswana to the other states we have examined. A strong expatriate presence masks a weak organizational structure within the public sector. Although political institutions have not been challenged by class or ethnic tensions, many fear they have been weakened by the domination of a self-serving organizational elite based in the civil service.[3] The development responsibilities of district councils have grown over the years, but efforts to devolve power to local authorities have met with limited success.

The Limits of Democratization

Increasingly, reformers in Africa are targeting political change and demanding a clear strategy for reforming central and local government organizations. Throughout the continent, national conventions and constituent assemblies are debating pluralism and multiparty democracy. The process of democratizing the public sector and policymaking requires the transfer of both administrative and political authority to intermediate as well as primary units of government.[4]

Concerns for political development are not new. The late 1950s and 1960s are rich with academic studies on the requirements for political stability and representative democracy.[5] Preconditions for the latter generally include high rates of urbanization, advanced development of voluntary organizations, overlapping and cross-cutting social affiliations, widespread literacy, adequate and equitably distributed personal incomes, and a shared sense of national identity.

Contemporary debates over governance reflect differences among this earlier generation of scholars. One position suggests that political stability, good management, and transparent decisionmaking are prerequisites to economic and social development.[6] For others, participatory democracy is the prerequisite for development.[7] Critics of governance ideas suggest that it is difficult to find correlations between governance principles and economic performance.[8]

A first step in the policy change process is achieving a proper balance of responsibilities between the public and private sectors. Economic reforms introduced under structural adjustment and conditionality often stumble because of governance and participation issues. Political instability often makes it difficult to define the boundaries between the public and the private sector, and it makes public-private partnership strategies difficult. More important, ideological differences continue to be significant in Africa, and many African elites remain ambiguous about the role of the private sector in a way that no longer characterizes Asia, Latin

America, or even much of Eastern Europe.

Pluralism efforts usually focus on electoral mechanisms. Elections, of course, are essential and serve to identify policy elites and governance mechanisms. Other forms of participatory democracy are also important. In many countries there is an absence of nongovernmental and community-based organizations and little participation by interest groups in the policy debate. Many countries still lack independent media. Elections without group representation and debate do not constitute democratic government. Promoting the role of NGOs and interest groups and increasing the independence of the media are part of an opening up of political space.

Promoting Democratization

In the promotion of democratization, measures to introduce political and economic accountability and improve information flows throughout society are crucial. Mechanisms must be developed and sustained to formalize communication between the public and private sectors and among the various sections of the economy as well as government units (horizontal and vertical).

African countries also must develop cross-cutting collaborative relationships across the institutional environment to encourage and promote debate, develop independent research and consultancy pools, strengthen internal management functions and policy analysis, and strengthen a sense of African ownership of the development process. Collaborative relationships are also needed between government and civil society for service delivery and popular participation in policy debates. These collaborative relationships need to be extended to the highest levels of government and may even include formalized approaches to policymaking between government and organized interests in a development corporatism model of decisionmaking.[9]

The Importance of Decentralization

Nigeria has experimented with federalism to lessen the dominance of central government on policymaking. Botswana, Kenya, and Nigeria continue to debate decentralization as a way to devolve power from national to regional, district, and subdistrict level councils. Although Ghana, Tanzania, and Zambia also have experimented with devolved political authority, all three states remain highly centralized.

Central-local relationships are important. Political and administrative reforms need to accompany economic reforms to decrease the absolute power and scope of the state. The decentralization of policymaking and policy implementation functions has the potential to widen the policy process to include a more participatory and pluralistic model of governance.

Throughout Africa, policy elites have been less than successful in decentralizing policymaking and administration. Several of the chapter authors argue that there must be an effective decentralization of the public sector to intermediate and primary units of governments for development management to occur.

Reform efforts should focus on both central and local government organizations. An upgrading of specialized policy units at the national level needs to be accompanied by similar efforts at the subnational level. Outside of government, efforts need to be made to upgrade and improve the performance of policy-oriented NGOs.[10] Issues of intergovernmental relationships and decentralization are mentioned by most of the chapter authors.

Both decentralization and pluralism have foundered on lack of resources (physical and human), a lack of skills, and the lack of political will to commit to devolved, participatory government. Political elites must make a commitment to a strategy for promoting and institutionalizing multiple centers of decisionmaking. The latter needs to be accompanied by commitments from host country and donor stakeholders to a strategy of organizational and geographical decentralization, which takes into account both local conditions and national priorities.

Policymaking and Institutional Development

Form Versus Substance

The failure of institutional development in African countries in the 1960s and 1970s was directly linked to the economic failures that became manifest in the 1980s. Policy reform offers a second try at institutional development in Africa. What is needed is an effective policymaking process that captures the most productive blend of grassroots, local, and national inputs into the public policy process through a strategic planning effort that: (1) includes all the major stakeholders—beneficiaries, target groups, and primary and secondary winners and losers; (2) considers the environmental threats and opportunities to successful implementation that are posed by various social, economic, and political factors; and (3) incorporates an appropriate institutional framework based on the requisite organizations and the rules, procedures, and laws that affect specific policies.[11] Employing a bottom-up strategy of development (the learning process approach) remains the most effective strategy by which private business and NGO community groups are able to generate initiatives.

Limitations on policy capacity have evolved within differing country conditions. The case studies in this book provide us with a number of insights into the policy process about which several conclusions can be drawn. Discussions about the nature of policymaking in each country have shown the extent to which the formal and constitutional aspects of governance differ from the reality of how policies are made. The economic, political, and administrative reform efforts under structural adjustment in Africa have met head on with this "form versus reality" problem. Although policy elites are often able to articulate a set of strategies in both political and economic terms, they are often not able to implement these goals. The form versus reality dichotomy has had an impact on both the political and administrative reform measures introduced, and it highlights the importance of country-specific environmental factors when change initiatives are planned.

The reform process itself is also responsible for some of the stumbling blocks that currently face policymakers in Africa. As several of our case studies illustrate, under structural adjustment and conditionality, reforms were externally initiated and they only partly involved indigenous stakeholders. Many policy reform initiatives that have failed have shown that expatriate advisers have an undue influence on decisionmaking and that their comings and goings often result in a lack of coordination and an insensitivity to local conditions.

There is a need to create a sense of African ownership of the reform process and policy development structures and processes. In order to get beyond the agenda of the donors, it is important to push, if not force, the concept of "donor coordination." This is an issue that is given much lip service, but little action on the part of donors, and it is the absence of such coordination that pulls the program officer and the LDC in a variety of directions.[12] Nongovernmental organizations are particularly susceptible to these tensions. As newly emergent donor recipients and with little experience in managing multiple agendas and sources of funding, NGO managers can be easily overwhelmed and lose sight of their own goals and objectives.

At the national level, as our case studies illustrate, a tendency for "ad-hocism" has emerged. Ghana, Nigeria, Kenya, and Tanzania have all experimented with reorganization to rationalize government functions at the center. A common approach has been the creation of committees and commissions for a specific purpose, but they often lack the institutional memory to allow for ongoing and strategic policy management.

Ad-hocism (through committees and commissions) has become a substitute for policy analysis units and the skilled individuals who would staff such units. It has also been used by political leaders who, for emotional, ideological, or patronage reasons, make decisions without the input of policy specialists and relevant stakeholders. The frequency of ad-hocism has led many of the authors to conclude that committees and commissions have become an "institutionalized" tool for policy management. The development of information gathering systems and consultative mechanisms to increase formalized, two-way communication flows is the most effective way to counter such tendencies.

Policy Change and Human Resource Development

Strategic management begins with the question, "What is the management task?" rather than who is responsible for administration. By placing task definition first a strategic management process can then begin to identify both governmental and nongovernmental entities whose participation and activities are essential to implementation of the policy. Clearly, in some cases one can identify nongovernmental groups with comparative advantage for taking on some tasks, and means can be determined to induce NGOs to share or assume responsibility for providing key services. There are also some things that must be done by government for planning or equity reasons.

In keeping with the task-oriented approach, human resource issues become important for addressing policy analysis and implementation capacity in both the public and the private sectors. All of our authors suggest that there is a need to establish a development-oriented civil service and NGO management at all levels of society. Although there will be continued dependence on the center for guidance, financial support, and planning services, implementation and mobilization must occur at the primary government level and can often be assisted by NGO activity.

Kenya and Botswana have continued to face problems of human resource capacity, particularly at the regional and local level. Specialized skills and experienced managers are also in short supply in Nigeria, Ghana, and Zambia. The shortage of human and financial resources continues to plague local efforts for autonomy. Even in Botswana, which has the most developed local government system in Africa, district councils are weak for this reason, and expatriates continue to dominate the policy process at all levels.

Many African countries are characterized by a small pool of local talent and a public sector that carries large numbers of unqualified and inexperienced personnel. In part, this is a reflection of the poor state of African education and training institutions where financial shortages and mismanagement have reduced the monies available for maintenance and upgrading. Any attempt to realistically address issues of human resource development must begin with efforts to strengthen these organizations.

Black, Coleman, and Stiffel have pointed out that there are several types of technical transfer that occur in strategic interventions in support of increasing management capacity. These technical transfers include tools, techniques, and technologies; skills in the analysis of the environment; principles of organization and management; and unstructured skills and analysis capacity.[13] The tools and techniques of administration transfer most rapidly and are not worth high levels of investment.

Unstructured skills are the most difficult to transfer because they require a "synthetic mode of thought . . . [in which] something explained is viewed as part of a larger system and is explained in terms of its role in that larger system."[14] At the upper levels of management, and for development management in general, it is the unstructured skills of judgment and analysis that make management an art rather than a science. In Africa, there is a need to establish a culture of management and organizational development principles that emphasizes management as an art as well as a science.

The assumption here (as with any generalization, there are, no doubt, some exceptions) is that creative development management (the synthetic mode of thought), for the most part, cannot be practiced by those who have not experienced the intellectual development that occurs with a university degree or its equivalent.[15] Thus, a future set of policy and managerial elites can develop only by strengthening education and training capacity in postgraduate university programs and high-level management development institutes.

Such assumptions have not always been made, especially in postcolonial Africa where ten years of basic education has been often considered adequate for even the most senior positions in the public and parastatal sectors[16]—and where aging civil servants retire to the private sector, often to front for international or minority community-dominated enterprises. The patterns that have emerged in African public management have not fostered the intellectual capacity that is critical for development management.

In the early years after independence, policymakers in many African countries used short "bridging" courses to train African administrators who were to replace colonial officials. This practice resulted in the placement of many poorly trained administrators in senior positions. Although in-service training has its role,[17] it should not be used as a substitute for long-term educational development.

Education and training are important components of policy reforms. Evidence from the case studies suggests that human resource development and the development of institutional memory are prerequisites to institutionalized policy management. The historical problems of training have been compounded by the limited opportunities that are available for continuous training and the near absence of orientation for senior officials assuming new positions.

Africa needs to develop a leadership cadre of managers for the twenty-first century, including the next generation of policy elites and an upper-level administrative cadre that can provide strategic management skills for all sectors of society. Leonard's important book on successful managers in Kenya[18] shows that this is possible.

Lessons for the Future

As a new cadre of LDC managers emerges and much of the attention once given to the public sector shifts to nongovernmental organizations, there is a pressing need to review the lessons learned from thirty years of technical assistance. An early argument remains valid—sustainability requires institutional development.

In a recent book, Osborne and Gaebler[19] called for the reinvention of government in the United States. They argued that what is needed is an "entrepreneurial government" where the focus is "not simply on public services, but on *catalyzing* all sectors—public, private, and voluntary—into action to solve their community's problems."[20] Reinvention strategies in international terms suggest the examination of new models of technical assistance and policy choices. While recognizing the differences between the public and the private sector, Osborne and Gaebler called for a strategy of replicating the entrepreneurialism of the private sector in government. The following four components of their model translate into a developing country setting.

Flexible financial management. Financial management systems require a fungible, flexible budget. Normal budget processes are wasteful because bureaucrats rush to spend all monies by the end of the year.

Agencies should focus on saving rather than spending funds. By allowing organizations to keep their surpluses every year, administrators will be encouraged to save rather than spend funds, resulting in more effective and efficient government—a government that is acting entrepreneurial. As our case studies show, financial management in a resource-poor LDC environment is a major challenge of development management.[21]

Employees as entrepreneurs. Whether inside government or out, employees need to be motivated to be entrepreneurial. One idea is to financially reward innovative employees by allowing them to keep a certain percentage of the savings/earnings that their innovations have provided. Entrepreneurial government models also call for decentralized authority and flattened hierarchies to promote creativity.

Reordering relationships. Two important sets of relationships can change under entrepreneurial government. First, the donor-recipient relationship is redefined, with donors becoming the customers of host country organizations.[22] Assuming agreement between the LDC and the host country, reordering donor-recipient relationships through more professional modes of operation places the donor in the position of a "client," who has contracted out for service deliverables. The donor as "client" can also act as "auditor" and provide feedback and criticism to those host country organizations that deliver agreed-upon services.

Second, in the domestic sphere, the government-client relationship can change with government treating their former clients as potential customers of government services. Both sets of relationships have historically been hierarchical in nature. Entrepreneurial government reorders traditional patterns of interaction, and with the change in perspective, group behavior can be modified. Particularly important is the emphasis entrepreneurial government places on empowering formerly subservient groups (donor recipients and LDC societies in this case) to make governance systems work more effectively and efficiently. In both instances, the government becomes an entrepreneurial agent producing services based on customer needs.

Steering versus rowing the process of government. Entrepreneurial government divides the process of governing into two parts: "steering" functions, where government acts as a catalyst and uses strategic planning to develop the "best" implementor, using some combination of government, private, and nongovernmental organizations; and "rowing" functions, where the government stays out of the operational side of the policy process. Entrepreneurial governments are active, but their responsibilities differ—the government plays a planning and facilitating role rather than an implementing role. In addition, government may also act as a catalyst in creating other steering organizations. A good example is government support (through direct funding or public endorsement) for the creation of NGOs whose major activities are strategic planning and coordination and who will draw in community-based organizations to empower citizens and provide a bottom-up process for setting priorities.[23]

Another LDC application of the "steering versus rowing" concept utilizes a foundation as a steering mechanism for policy planning and management. The major advantage of a foundation is that it allows for an interface with government organizations, NGOs, and the private sector. Other advantages include: (1) the provision of multiple types of funding through grants and contracts; (2) the ability to act as a coordinating mechanism facilitating the formation of multiple partnerships and coalitions among government organizations, the private sector, and NGO and donor organizations; (3) the ability to perform as a development agency expanding the potential pool of funding available through the introduction of matching funds (or challenge grants); and (4) by not being connected either to the government or the private sector, the foundation is seen by all stakeholders as independent. In South Africa, the foundation model is being applied to a number of development efforts as the country moves toward majority rule.[24]

Institutional Development Within the Foundation Approach

If donor technical assistance targets the creation of real opportunities for collaborative efforts to produce high-quality project proposals and to promote learning of the necessary skills to develop such proposals, a foundation approach could go a long way toward the creation of a learning-process model that results in sustainability. Working through a foundation, technical assistance agencies can use request-for-proposal procedures and unsolicited proposals as mechanisms to fund development activities.

Developing proposals for a foundation requires a prospective NGO or government recipient to demonstrate organizational capacity to implement the project. Long before grantee funds or a contract is awarded, a collaborative and interactive relationship can develop between donor and recipient, with clear expectations about the project and its goals. Moreover, the board and committee members of recipient organizations can also be encouraged to participate in the process along with the LDC program manager, enhancing the opportunities for capacity building. NGO/PVO organization structures, with the board mandated with policy responsibilities and secretariats assuming the day-to-day administrative duties, require close teamwork and a clear understanding about where the organization is headed in order to be successful. The foundation approach has the potential to bring all the relevant stakeholders into the process at an early stage.

There is some evidence that the new Clinton administration is beginning to apply some of the principles of entrepreneurialism to the federal government. As the literature on privatization and public-private partnerships illustrates, what begins as domestic policy in North America and Europe often enters the policy debate on international development efforts.[25] With a reorganization of the U.S. Agency for International Development in the cards, there is likely to be much discussion of entrepreneurial government in technical assistance circles over the next several years.

Conclusion

Much remains to be done to define the relationship between sustainability and institutional development. A strategy to build implementation and management capacity must focus on sustainability factors in human resource development, organizational development, and overall education and training strategies. Such a strategy must be accompanied by efforts to upgrade local education and training institutions through collaborative models at the national and regional level and through processes that produce a "spread effect" in terms of policy analysis and policy management.

In Africa, organizational development and capacity building for strategic management require the development of suitable technical assistance and host country participating agency procedures and communication processes.[26] Recipients need to be able to manage their relationship with donors, and donors need to professionalize their relationships with recipients. Both sides of the relationship can be improved by using contracting-out mechanisms to separate human resource development activities from service delivery activities.

Implementation is important. Improving planning and policy analysis capacity does not in and of itself increase the capacity of government to achieve its goals. Sustainability factors that improve capacity include a focus on human resource development, organizational development, and overall education and training strategies. In particular, the development of management skills improves capacity and increases the potential for sustainability of programs and policies. While many aspects of implementation require technical skills, it must be remembered that management is an art as well as a science, and that some management courses must emphasize problem solving from an analytical perspective.

A major focus of technical assistance should be the intersection between government and the private sector because the implementation of policy change requires the development of partnership arrangements between the two.[27] At issue is the need to clarify perceived interest conflicts and their relationship to policy objectives and related strategic management issues. Such partnerships should be considered as a part of the public policy arena.[28] The models vary and achieving a balance must be country specific, based upon the historical context of the country and the nature of interest groups that operate within the developing polity.

Successful partnerships require a planning process that is task oriented, financially realistic, and capacity based. The development of partnership arrangements also affects donor strategies, which should include the identification of appropriate strategies and approaches to the privatization of government functions,[29] and the effective and efficient reform of those functions that remain in the public sector. In particular, privatization strategies should include measures to enhance financial analysis capacity to ensure that public monopolies do not become private monopolies. Both contractor service organizations and research institutes should be given a monitoring responsibility to track the social and economic costs of policy reforms. The design and introduction of effective monitoring systems within government are also necessary to assess the effects of policy reforms on the socioeconomic patterns at the macrolevel.

Sustainability and replicability are the keys to a successful donor-supported design and implementation strategy and an on-going assessment process for technical assistance. As our case studies show, African development managers are increasingly concerned to develop the capacity to insure the sustainability of project and program benefits beyond the limited time horizon of the donor's direct involvement.[30]

At issue is the way in which the public-private balance is achieved and the extent to which the partnership reflects development priorities. A strategic planning process that includes all of the major stakeholders of society, including potential beneficiaries and target groups as well as potential winners and losers in the development process, is fundamental in defining the partnership arrangement. Negotiating policies for development in this setting should be part of a broader set of negotiations that can establish the principles of governance throughout Africa.

Notes

1. Robert Klitgaard, *Tropical Gangsters: One Man's Experience with Development and Decadence in Deepest Africa* (New York: Basic Books, 1990).
2. Henry Bienen, *Kenya: The Politics of Participation and Control* (Princeton, N.J.: Princeton University Press, 1974).
3. Louis A. Picard, "Bureaucrats, Cattle and Public Policy: Land Tenure Changes in Botswana," *Comparative Political Studies*, vol. 13, no. 3 (October 1980), pp. 313–356.
4. George Peterson, "Decentralization and Democratic Governance: A Review of Latin American Experience and Lessons for Sub-Saharan Africa" (paper prepared for the Office of Housing and Urban Programs, U.S. Agency for International Development, Washington, D.C., Urban Institute, March 1991).
5. See Lucian W. Pye, *Aspects of Political Development* (Boston: Little, Brown, 1966), and the Series on Political Development of Princeton University Press (Princeton, N.J.): *Communications and Political Development*, ed. Lucian W. Pye (1963); *Bureaucracy and Political Development*, ed. Joseph LaPalombara (1963); *Political Modernization in Japan and Turkey*, ed. Robert E. Ward and Dankwart A. Rustow (1964); *Education and Political Development*, ed. James S. Coleman (1965); *Political Culture and Political Development*, ed. Lucian W. Pye and Sidney Verba (1965); *Political Parties and Political Development*, ed. Joseph LaPalombara and Myron Weiner (1966); and *Crises in Political Development*, ed. Leonard Binder et al. (1971).
6. See *Managing Development: The Governance Dimension: A Discussion Paper* (Washington, D.C.: The World Bank, August 29, 1991) for a discussion of this view. Samuel Huntington argued that political order rather than participation was a key factor in promoting social and economic change. See his *Political Order in Changing Societies* (New Haven, Conn.: Yale University Press, 1968). A later book with Joan M. Nelson maintained that political participation can be a by-product of economic development. See their *No Easy Choice: Political Participation in Developing Countries* (Cambridge, Mass.: Harvard University Press, 1976). For a survey of these issues see Monte Palmer, *Dilemmas of Political Development* (Itasca, Ill.: F. E. Peacock Publishers, 1989).
7. See Robert Charlick, "Governance Working Paper" (prepared for the A.I.D. Africa Bureau under the Africa Bureau Democracy and Governance Program, Burlington, Vt., Associates in Rural Development, January 1992).
8. See Deborah Brautigam, *Governance and Economy: A Review*, Policy Research Working Paper (Washington, D.C.: The World Bank, December, 1991). See also Joan M. Nelson, ed., *Economic Crisis and Policy Choice: The Politics of Adjustment in the Third World* (Princeton, N.J.: Princeton University Press, 1990), for a discussion of this issue.
9. We are grateful to Maureen Widzgowski for this point. See her

"Structural Adjustment and the Political Economy of Mexico: The Prospects for Continued Wage Repression in the 1990s" (unpublished paper, Pittsburgh, 1992). See also Michele Garrity and Louis A. Picard, "Organized Interests, the State, and the Public Policy Process: An Assessment of Jamaican Business Associations," *Journal of Developing Areas*, vol. 25 (April 1991), pp. 369–394, for an elaboration of this point.

10. Strengthening state institutions includes the upgrading and development of specialized policy units capable of delivering the kind of policy analysis needed to make effective development decisions. To achieve sectoral balance and pluralist governance patterns requires policy parallelism in implementing policy change. Parallelism involves the pairing of related public sector and private sector organizations that are concerned with similar policies and their implementation. Pairing suggests that if training or the development of a policy analysis capacity to increase the capacity of a government organization occurs, the need for sectoral balance (avoiding overstrong government) requires increasing the capacity of private sector organizations that interact with the state. For example, if management implementation skills in a particular part of the public sector are increased, then private sector skills should also be upgraded. Parallelism is an effective way of ensuring public-private sector balance in terms of capacity building. Thus, support for an export promotion council in Country X to strengthen international trade would require strengthening of a nongovernmental exporters association at the same time.

11. Derick W. Brinkerhoff, *Improving Development Program Performance: Guidelines for Managers* (Boulder, Colo.: Lynne Rienner Publishers, 1991). Our guidelines have incorporated Brinkerhoff's framework for "looking out, looking in, looking ahead" ideas.

12. India comes to mind as a country that takes a very strong management role vis-à-vis donors.

13. Picard has noted four types of administration in LDCs (maintenance administration, scaffolding administration, praetorian administration, and development administration). Louis A. Picard, *Administrative Attitudes and Time: Role Changes in Bechuanaland and Botswana*, SICA Occasional Paper Series, 2nd series, no. 7 (Austin, Tex.: Section on International and Comparative Administration, American Society for Public Administration, 1985), p. 7. General management at the upper levels of an organization, and development administration generally, is different than maintenance administration at the middle and lower levels. These, in turn, differ from sectoral management skills (health, education, agriculture, transport, and marketing). See also Joseph Black, James S. Coleman, and Laurence D. Stiffel, eds., *Education and Training for Public Sector Management in the Developing Countries* (New York: Rockefeller Foundation, March 1977), p. 44.

14. Black et al., *Education and Training for Public Sector Management*, p.44.

15. It is, of course, not the bits of paper from a university that allows for creative thinking and judgment. Rather it is the nature of the experience that some, not all, receive in a university-based experience that is important. Certainly there are people without a university experience that have rich analytical experience and through experience and intellect have had an intellectual development process that is analogous to the best of those who attend university. However, the university experience is the most likely route to unbounded analytical thinking.

16. Wyn Reilly made this point. See his *Training Administrators for*

Development (London: Heineman, 1979).

17. In-service training is required to transfer the techniques of policy analysis, organization management, development planning, and management for the public, parastatal, and private sectors. Institutes of business management, administration, and development management need to include internal management skills.

18. David K. Leonard, *African Successes: Four Public Managers of Kenyan Rural Development* (Berkeley: University of California Press, 1991), p. 18.

19. David Osborne and Ted Gaebler, *Reinventing Government: How the Entrepreneurial Spirit Is Transforming the Public Sector* (Reading, Mass.: Addison-Wesley, 1992).

20. Ibid., p. 20.

21. Naomi Caiden and Aaron Wildavsky, *Planning and Budgeting in Poor Countries* (New York: John Wiley & Sons, 1974).

22. Donors as "customers" or "clients" could occur by introducing competition within the authorization process and including public sector organizations in request-for-proposal (RFP) bids. Donor-recipient relationships would also change because entrepreneurial government introduces an ongoing assessment into them. LDC managers are likely to see the project as an integral part of an already existing program. Project designers need to allow for continual evaluation by both the donor and host country officials and to provide for the possibility of replication after the project ends. LDC program managers are painfully aware that donor-sponsored project interventions often do not successfully pursue these goals. See John D. Montgomery, *The Politics of Foreign Aid: American Experience in Southeast Asia* (New York: Praeger, 1962).

23. A good illustration of this support in practice has been occurring in South Africa where "umbrella" NGOs are supporting the development of widely dispersed community-based organizations. The South African experience differs only in that these umbrella organizations currently work without the support of government. With the transition to majority rule, it is anticipated that the new government will rely extensively on such mechanisms to meet the heavy demands of citizens from forty-odd years of apartheid.

24. For example, see Foundation for Public Management and Development, *Action Plan, April 1–August 1, 1992* (Johannesburg: FPMD, 1992). The Educational Opportunity Council is another such organization that is likely to coordinate technical assistance for higher education in South Africa.

25. Clyde Mitchell-Weaver and Brenda Manning, "Public-Private Partnerships in Third World Development: A Conceptual Overview," *Studies in Comparative International Development*, vol. 26, no. 4 (Winter 1991–1992), pp. 45–67.

26. Where possible, technical assistance could include in its programs the teaching of donor recipient concepts and procedures to host country cooperants. Donor management and procedures and appropriate client-donor relationships are thus far a neglected area in management training and education.

27. See Mitchell-Weaver and Manning, "Public-Private Partnerships," pp. 43–65.

28. This section, in part, is taken from Louis A. Picard, "Implementing Policy Change and the Public/Private Interface" (unpublished paper, Washington, D.C., January 14, 1992).

29. See, for example, Keith Marsden, *African Entrepreneurs: Pioneers of Development*, International Finance Corporation Discussion Paper no. 9 (Washington, D.C.: The World Bank, 1990); *Developing the Private Sector: The World Bank's Experience and Approach* (Washington, D.C.: The World Bank, 1990); *Prospects for the Business Sector in Developing Countries*, International Finance Corporation Discussion Paper no. 3 (Washington, D.C.: The World Bank, 1989); and Guy P. Pfeffermann, *Private Business in Developing Countries: Improved Prospects*, International Finance Corporation Discussion Paper no. 1 (Washington, D.C.: The World Bank, 1988).

30. Louise G. White, *Creating Opportunities for Change: Approaches to Managing Development Programs* (Boulder, Colo.: Lynne Rienner Publishers, 1987), p. 6. UNDP has transformed its efforts from a project to a program basis.

Index

About the Editors
and Contributors

Louis A. Picard is associate professor at the Graduate School of Public and International Affairs, University of Pittsburgh. His many publications include *The Politics of Development in Botswana* and *South Africa in Southern Africa* (with Edmond J. Keller).

Michele Garrity is the managing director of P & G Associates, a development management consulting firm. She is the author of "Organized Interests, the State, and the Public Policy Process" (with Louis A. Picard), *Journal of Developing Areas* (1991), and *Sanctions Against South Africa* (with Louis A. Picard and Veronique Lozach).

H. Akuoko-Frimpong is acting director of the Management Development and Productivity Institute in Accra, Ghana.

Mulenga C. Bwalya is principal, National Institute of Public Administration, Lusaka, Zambia.

Ason Bur is deputy governor, Benue State Government, Makurdi, Nigeria.

Athumani J. Liviga is senior lecturer of political studies, University of Dar es Salaam, Tanzania, and is currently affiliated with the Graduate School of Public and International Affairs, University of Pittsburgh.

Gatian F. Lungu is professor of public administration at the University of Western Cape, Cape Town, South Africa.

Rwekaza S. Mukandala is senior lecturer of political studies at the University of Dar es Salaam, Tanzania.

Elvidge G. M. Mhlauli is associate director of the Directorate of Public Service Management, Gaborone, Botswana.

Walter O. Oyugi is professor of political science at the University of Nairobi, Nairobi, Kenya.

Keshav C. Sharma is professor and chair of the Department of Political and Administrative Studies, University of Botswana.

William Shellukindo is principal secretary, Civil Service Department, Office of the President, Dar es Salaam, Tanzania.

Ali D. Yahaya is secretary general of the African Association of Public Administration and Management, Nairobi, Kenya.

About the Book

Thirty years of donor-supported development programs in Africa have shown that the intricacies of policy content have usually won out over the institutional requirements necessary for effective and efficient government. Consequently, administrative and managerial capacity has been declining rather than improving in much of the continent, and the introduction of structural adjustment policies has tended to compound the problem. Reform initiatives to strengthen weak markets and bolster weak states have typically ignored the critical institutional imperatives necessary for generating vibrant markets and a viable governance process.

This book revisits issues of sustainable development and capacity building, focusing on the experiences of African researchers and practitioners. The authors—representing the public and nongovernmental sectors as well as the donor community—concentrate on four themes: good governance requires an appropriate balance of responsibilities between the public and private sectors; pluralism and decentralization are fundamental to sustainability; management capacity is the weak link in development programs; and institution building is directly linked to sustainability. The case studies cover Ghana, Nigeria, Zambia, Tanzania, Kenya, and Botswana.